# On→the→Go Bags

## 15 Handmade Purses, Totes & Organizers

Unique Projects to Sew
from Today's Modern Designers

Lindsay Conner and Janelle MacKay

stash BOOKS.

*an imprint of C&T Publishing*

Text copyright © 2015 by Lindsay Conner and Janelle MacKay

Photography and artwork copyright © 2015 by C&T Publishing, Inc.

Publisher: Amy Marson

Creative Director: Gailen Runge

Art Director/Cover Designer: Kristy Zacharias

Editor: Liz Aneloski

Technical Editors: Debbie Rodgers and Amanda Siegfried

Book Designer: April Mostek

Production Coordinators: Jenny Davis and Freesia Pearson Blizard

Production Editor: Alice Mace Nakanishi

Illustrator: Aliza Shalit

Photo Assistants: Mary Peyton Peppo and Sarah Frost

Style photography by Nissa Brehmer and instructional photography by Diane Pedersen, unless otherwise noted

Published by Stash Books, an imprint of C&T Publishing, Inc., P.O. Box 1456, Lafayette, CA 94549

Library of Congress Cataloging-in-Publication Data

Conner, Lindsay, 1983-

 On the go bags : 15 handmade purses, totes & organizers : unique projects to sew from today's modern designers / Lindsay Conner and Janelle MacKay.

   pages cm

ISBN 978-1-61745-130-0 (soft cover)

1. Bags. 2. Handbags. 3. Sewing. I. MacKay, Janelle, 1971- II. Title.

TT667.C64 2015

646.4'8--dc23

                        2015014708

Printed in China

10 9 8 7 6 5 4 3 2 1

# Contents

# Dedication

*Thank you to all the people in my life who've graciously allowed me the time, space, and freedom to create. My husband, Matt, is my biggest fan and the instigator behind all my best ideas. My parents have fielded numerous frantic phone calls and loved every minute of grandparenting. And little Elliot—who has watched me lose my cell phone, wallet, keys, and groceries— thank you for making me realize that I need a better bag to hold all your junk. I love you.*

*—Lindsay*

*This book is dedicated to my dear mom, who, when I was young, encouraged me to use my hands and heart to create things that I could love making and be proud of. She taught me to knit, crochet, embroider, cross-stitch, and best of all, to use a sewing machine. This book is also dedicated to my amazing husband, for all his support and encouragement. Mike, thank you for putting up with all my creative messes, and I owe you an apology for not paying attention when my mom was teaching me to cook.*

*—Janelle*

# Acknowledgments

First of all, thank you to the publishing team at C&T for believing in us and spending countless hours turning this project into a bound book. It has been a pleasure to work with our book team: Liz Aneloski, Debbie Rodgers, Amanda Siegfried, Kristy Zacharias, April Mostek, Jenny Davis, Freesia Pearson Blizard, and Alice Mace Nakanishi. Without the creativity and dedication of our amazing contributors, this book would not be possible. We also thank our meticulous pattern testers and designers: Kate Alicea, Jennifer Bryant, Betty Canfield, Natalie Cox, Candis Gengler, Cindy Guch, Sue Kim, Tracey Lipman, Gwen Lockwood, Katie Mehta, Laurel Notturno, Jenny Parker, Angela Pingel, Marcia Reel, Lindsey Rion, Jennifer Savelio, Simone Symonds, Maria A. Vazquez, and Nicole Young. Last but not least, thank you to Baby Lock sewing machines and to all the companies who supported this project by generously providing materials to bring our designs to life (see Resources, page 143).

# Introduction

Does it feel like you always have somewhere to be? Whether you're packing for vacation, dropping off the kids at school, or running a quick errand on the way to work, your life is in a constant state of motion.

Your story is like all of ours. It's a story of learning to breathe in the midst of a crazy day. It's a story of losing your cell phone, and of watching the shopping cart roll down the parking lot while you dig for your keys.

But it's also a story of making, learning, and growing. It's about the innate feeling of accomplishment when someone sees your bag and asks, "Did you make that?" It's the sense of mastery that comes with sewing your own bags, fulfilling your human desire to create.

Flip through these pages and you'll discover fifteen innovative patterns for bags and organizers to make life easier when you're on the go. Your favorite bag designers and popular bloggers have contributed unique, handmade organizers for specific purposes, from protecting your iPad to changing purses in an instant. Beyond the basic tote or zippered pouch, you'll learn to make several styles of pockets and straps; install purse hardware, zippers, elastic, and cording; apply interfacing and stabilizers; and pair designer fabrics with unusual materials like vinyl and mesh.

Start with one of the beginner-friendly patterns, and then challenge yourself with an intermediate or advanced bag. You'll learn to sew stylish bags and organizers that will do more than just look pretty on a shelf—they'll actually make your life easier!

As an added bonus, you'll see that most bags in this book have dual purposes, making them incredibly versatile and practical to sew. For instance, a coupon organizer not only straps onto the grocery cart but also hooks onto the stroller to carry a child's drink and snack (see Cart or Stroller Caddy, page 51).

Work through the projects and you'll gain confidence in your technique, as you sew useful and really unique bags and organizers to fit your on-the-go lifestyle. We hope each bag also helps you nurture your inner maker, allowing you a moment to grow into your creative self.

With each stitch, we wish you a retreat from your crazy life. There's always somewhere you have to be. But wherever you are coming from or going to, your handmade bag can go with you. It's a gentle reminder that you are creative, accomplished, and uniquely you. Happy travels, and happy sewing!

# Techniques

## Cutting with a Rotary Cutter

This book includes both pullout pattern pages and rotary cutting instructions. Rotary cutting instructions allow bag makers to use fast and accurate cutting skills, which yield fabric pieces with straight, square, and precise edges. For some traditional bag makers, this method can be a daunting task if they are unfamiliar with it, but after using the rotary cutting instructions, most bag makers decide they love the precision, accuracy, and professional results. You can cut several layers at a time with no drawing or template making required. When you are rotary cutting, make sure you cut your rectangles on the straight grain of the fabric and label all your pieces.

## Pattern Pieces

Some of the projects in this book refer to pattern pieces that are included on the two-sided pullout pattern page at the end of the book. These pattern pieces are full size and include seam allowances. Make your own pattern pieces by tracing your required piece onto tracing paper, template plastic, or lightweight interfacing. You could also use dressmaker's carbon paper and a tracing wheel to transfer the cutting lines onto fabric. Remember to cut all the notches and transfer all the placement markings.

# Curved Corners

Some rectangular fabric pieces will require curved corners, so we have provided a set of corner patterns. Although you may choose to eyeball your curves and cut them freehand with a rotary cutter, you may wish to trace the required corner pattern onto a piece of paper or template plastic before rounding the corners of your fabric. To use corner templates, place the curved template on the corner of the fabric piece and trace with a pen and cut, or simply cut along the curve with your rotary cutter. Flip the template over and repeat for the opposite corner.

**Tip**

To save time, grab a cup or saucer from the kitchen and try the curve of the top rim on the required template to find a size that matches.

# Fusible Interfacings, Fleece, and Stabilizers

Always refer to the manufacturer's directions to attach any fusible interfacings, stabilizers, or fleece, but here are a few key tricks and tips to make the process go smoothly.

- Select interfacing that is appropriate for the weight of the fabric you are using. Use light- to medium-weight interfacing for light- to medium-weight fabrics, and medium- to heavyweight interfacing for medium- to heavyweight fabrics. A heavyweight interfacing on a lightweight fabric will create a stiff, papery fabric that's prone to creases and bubbles. A very lightweight interfacing will not be a great help to heavier fabrics. Woven interfacing is a bag maker's favorite because it provides structure to the fabric and doesn't feel stiff and crinkly.

- Choose the right heat setting on your iron for the fabric you are using. For a lighter fabric or fabric that will scorch or burn with a higher heat setting, you will need to choose an interfacing that will adhere at a lower temperature. (These are generally the lightweight interfacings.) Always use a pressing cloth with these kinds of fabrics when fusing. Medium- to heavyweight interfacings need higher heat to fuse and are more appropriate for fabrics that can handle high temperatures and steam. When pressing, choose a lower setting first. If you don't have success in about 5 or 6 seconds, increase the heat in increments.

- Always press your fabric before cutting pattern pieces and applying the interfacing. This will not only help to remove wrinkles but can also help preshrink your fabric if it is prone to shrinking, particularly if you use steam.

- Trim the interfacing ¼″ to ½″ smaller on all sides than the fabric piece you are fusing it to. This will not only keep the interfacing out of your seam allowances and reduce bulk in the seams, but also save your ironing board from any adhesive that might sneak over the edges if the interfacing is too large.

- Apply the adhesive side of the interfacing to the wrong side of the fabric piece you are fusing to. This might seem like basic instruction, but if you've had to remove that sticky interfacing adhesive off of your iron a time or two, you'll know it's probably the most important step!

- Starting at one corner, press and count for 8–10 seconds, lift the iron, and press down again, overlapping onto the area you just pressed. Check to see if your interfacing is fusing to the fabric and adjust the temperature or length of time you are pressing as needed. Avoid sliding the iron on the surface, because this could stretch your fabric pieces out of shape.

## Tip ←

**Have you ever noticed large bubbles or circles of interfacing that are not getting fused down to your fabric? Have a look at the bottom of your iron to see how big your steam holes are. Large steam holes or gaps on the bottom of your iron create areas that will not get fused down. Try to find an iron with small steam holes, and make sure you are overlapping as you go to press these areas down. That is why overlapping is so important!**

- Steam! Most interfacings like woven interfacing, fusible fleece, and heavy stabilizers need steam, steam, and more steam to create proper adhesion.

- After you are done fusing, turn your fabric over, so the right side is up, and press out any wrinkles or bubbles. Either let the fabric stay in place to cool or lift it up and lay it on a flat surface for a few moments. If you manipulate it while it is cooling, it could stretch out of shape.

# Secure Thread Ends

## Backstitching

Backstitching at the starts and stops of seams is one way to make sure your stitches don't unravel, and burying your thread ends is the way to make sure your topstitching is both secure from unraveling and clean and professional looking.

To backstitch, or lock your stitches at the start of a seam, hold your bobbin and top thread in your left hand when you start. Stitch three stitches forward, three stitches back, and then carry on forward to the end of your seam. When you reach the end, stitch back three stitches and then forward again.

## Pull the Bobbin Thread to the Back and Tie Off

Sometimes on your bag strap or other topstitching, you don't want to see the ends of your thread where they were trimmed off and are now sticking up on your beautiful topstitching. The solution to this is to pull your bobbin thread to the back of your project. Simply turn your project over so you can see the back, and pull the bobbin thread until a loop of top thread pops through to the back. Use a pin to hook that loop and pull the top thread to the back. Tie the threads to secure.

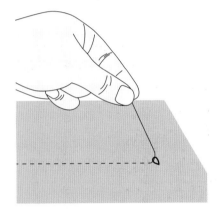

If your two thread ends are now tied together on the back but are on a bag element that will be seen, such as a strap, you can bury them in the fabric. Simply thread them onto a needle and poke down into the fabric right beside the knot. Slip the needle between the fabric layers, so it is neither on the front nor on the back, and come back up about 1″ away. Pull the thread slightly so that it is tight, snip the thread next to the fabric, and let it sink back down between the layers.

# Making Bag Straps

Most of the projects in this book use the popular 4-fold strap method. It's a quick and easy way to make a sturdy, professional-looking bag strap that, with its four layers, provides its own interfacing for thickness. Sometimes when using lighter cottons, a layer of interfacing or fusible fleece inside the strap is needed to create some extra stiffness. The strap can be used with rings and buckles or may be sewn directly onto a bag exterior.

## 4-Fold Open-End Strap

Open-end straps have raw edges and are often used when the strap ends will be sewn into the seam, such as a shoulder strap or strap tabs. Use the provided measurements given in the project instructions included in this book and the following directions to make your bag strap. If you are creating a bag strap for your own project, you will need to take the desired width of the bag strap you need and multiply that by 4 to get the width of fabric required, and the length of the strap you want plus any seam allowances at the ends to get the length of fabric required.

**1.** Fold the entire strap in half lengthwise with the wrong sides together and press. *Figure A*

**2.** Open the strap again, fold the outside edges toward the center fold mark, and press. *Figure B*

**3.** Refold the entire strip in half once again, meeting the folded edges together, and press. *Figure C*

**4.** Topstitch around all 4 sides, using a long stitch length and staying about ⅛˝ from the edges. Continue topstitching the strap in your preferred style to match the rest of your project. *Figure D*

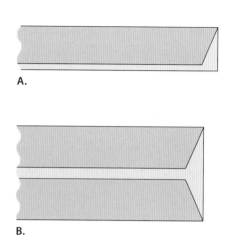

**A.**

**B.**

**C.**

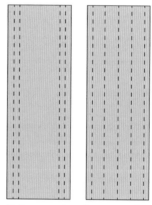

**D.** Some options for top-stitching your straps

## Tips ←

- If you are using quilting cottons, you may want to add strength and a bit of structure to your bag strap. Do this by fusing a piece of light- to medium-weight interfacing in one or both of the center quarters of the strap. Cut interfacing that is ¼ or ½ of the width of the original fabric strip.

- If you find that the top layer is sliding when you are stitching, try pinning down the open side before you make your first stitches. Pin every 3″ or so. If you have a material that is sliding quite a bit on itself, use a walking foot or wash-away double-sided tape to keep it in place.

## 4-Fold Closed-End Strap

Closed-end straps are most often used when the end of the bag straps will be seen, such as when bag straps are folded over a strap ring or when they are sewn to the outside exterior of a bag. In these cases, you will not want to see the raw edges on the end of a bag strap.

**1.** To make a 4-Fold Closed-End Strap, use the strip of fabric required in your project instructions and first press both short ends of the strap over ¼″ to the wrong side of the fabric.

**2.** Follow 4-Fold Open-End Strap, Steps 1–4 (page 10), to finish making your closed-end strap.

## Adjustable Strap

**1.** Thread the end of a closed-end strap through the adjustable slider, folding it over the middle bar and then back onto itself. Sew a box with an X through the middle to secure. *Figure A*

**2.** With the wrong side of the adjustable slider facing up, thread the other end of the strap through one of the bag rings on either a strap extender, a side strap tab, or a swivel snap hook (lobster hook), depending on which you are using, and then back through the adjustable slider. *Figures B–D*

**3.** Attach the free end of the strap either right onto the opening of a bag, onto another bag ring, or onto another swivel snap hook, by sewing a box with an X through the middle to secure. *Figures E–G*

**A.**

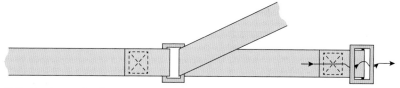

**B.** End to strap extender

**C.** End to side strap tab

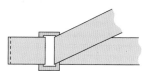

**D.** End to swivel snap hook

**E.** End to other side of bag

**F.** End to another bag ring

**G.** End to another swivel snap hook

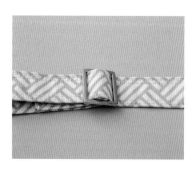

# Insert Bag Clasps and Closures

## Magnetic Snap

**1.** Cut a 1½″ × 1½″ square of one-sided, fusible heavyweight interfacing or stabilizer (such as Pellon Peltex 71F). Find the center of the square and mark this with a cross or dot.

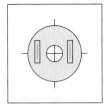

**A.**

**2.** If the directions call for centering the magnetic snap, this is easily done by folding the fabric piece in half vertically to find the center top, or in quarters to find the exact center of the fabric piece. Press the interfacing or stabilizer square in place on the wrong side of the fabric, using a pressing cloth and steam setting.

**3.** Center the provided washer over the center mark and draw in the 2 rectangular cutting lines. *Figure A*

**B.**

**4.** Using a seam ripper or sharp-pointed scissors, cut through the 2 drawn marks where the prongs will poke through. *Figure B*

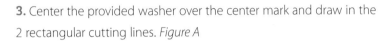

## Tip

**It is very important that you don't cut your slots for the snap prongs too big. If you do, your snap will be loose. In fact, always make them a bit smaller than the drawn lines, because the material will stretch to make room for them. Use seam sealant or fray-stopping liquid on the slits you cut to prevent fraying.**

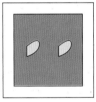

**C.**

**5.** Push one of the magnetic snap halves through from the *right side* of the fabric.

**6.** Cut a couple of squares from thick fleece, batting, or felt to put over the prongs on the back of each snap. This will make your snap fit nice and tight. Clip a couple slits where the prongs will go through and slide the squares on. *Figure C*

**7.** Place something soft under the magnet such as felt or folded fabric, so that the magnet front won't get scratched on your table. Place the washer over the prongs and, while pushing down very firmly, bend your prongs outward one at a time using a heavy tool, such as a large flat screwdriver.

> ### NOTE
> The prongs on the back of the snap could also be folded inward, which is sometimes suggested in patterns, because this could prevent the metal prong ends from wearing through the fabric. This is also a good idea if you are working with a small item and you don't have room for the prongs to stick out to each side. But if you need the snap to lie a bit flatter, perhaps for a handbag flap or wallet, we suggest folding them outward. Gluing or fusing a square of felt or batting over the back side of the snap to cover the prongs is a great way to prevent the prongs from rubbing through the bag lining.

## Purse Lock

Shiny metal purse locks, sometimes called turn locks or twist locks, come in all shapes, sizes, and finishes. They add a professional touch to your bag or purse that can really take it to the next level. You can find complete instructions to add a metal turn lock in the project instructions for the *Airport Sling* (page 109).

# Bias Binding and Piping

Although both prepackaged bias binding and piping are available at most fabric stores, sometimes it's nice to add that special touch with some handmade piping or binding that coordinates nicely with the project you are making. Cute stripes, polka dots, and prints make gorgeous, one-of-a kind trim, and they are not difficult to make!

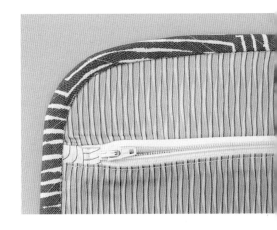

## Double-Layer Bias Binding

Bias binding can be made a few different ways, depending on your project. A few projects in this book require *double-layer bias binding*, sometimes called *quilt binding* or *French fold binding*, as an edge-finishing technique, so we'll focus on this method.

To make double-layer bias binding, you will need to decide on the width of binding you need for your project and multiply that by 6. For instance, if you want your finished bias tape binding to be ½˝ wide, you will need to cut a bias strip that is 3˝ wide. Refer to your materials and supplies list in your project instructions to determine the finished width required.

**1.** Make double-layer bias binding by cutting strips of fabric on the bias. (Bias-cut binding works much better for going around curves than straight-cut binding because it is slightly stretchy.) Fold a large rectangle of fabric so that the lengthwise grain is running parallel to the crosswise grain, creating a fold at a 45° angle across the fabric. Cut this fold to create an edge from which to measure and cut your strips. Continue cutting strips across the bias at your desired width. *Figure A*

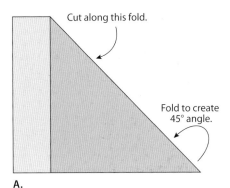

Cut along this fold.

Fold to create 45° angle.

**A.**

**2.** Join the strips to make one long strip that will fit the length or perimeter of your project. With *right sides together*, overlap the strips at a 90° angle. If the ends of the strips are already at a 45° angle, have the ends of each strip extend past the other piece by ¼˝. Using a ¼˝ seam allowance, stitch diagonally across from corner to corner. Trim the seam allowance to ¼˝. Press the seams open. *Figures B & C*

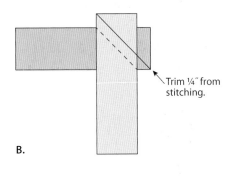

Trim ¼˝ from stitching.

**B.**

**3.** Press the entire strip in half lengthwise with wrong sides together.

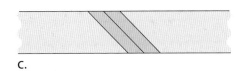

**C.**

# Attaching Bias Binding

**1.** With the raw edges even, pin the binding to the front edge of the piece, gently stretching it around any curves.

**2.** Stitch in place, using the seam allowance given in the specific project.

**3.** If you are binding something where the ends don't need to be joined together, simply sew from end to end. If you need to join the ends, start sewing 2″ from the start of the binding and then stop about 2½″ before the end. Make sure the end of the binding overlaps the start by ½″ and trim off evenly.

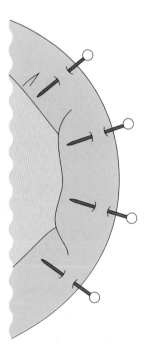

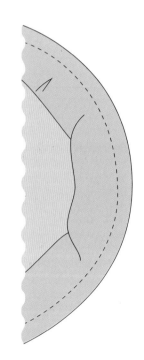

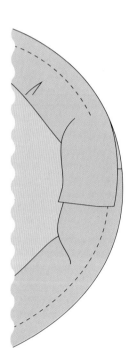

**4.** Pull the 2 ends of the binding together, so that they meet together evenly. With *right sides facing*, pinch the ends together, pulling them away from the project, and pin the ends together. Stitch the bias binding ends together. Press the seam open. Pin the joined bias binding down onto the edge of the project and stitch in place.

**5.** Wrap the bias tape around to the back side and press the seam flat. Pin in the seam to secure. Make sure it is pulled over just past the stitching line you made to attach it.

**6.** Using a thread color to match your front fabric for the top thread and a thread color to match your binding in the bobbin, and working from the front side, stitch in-the-ditch down the inside edge of the bias tape, catching the binding edge that is on the other side. If preferred, you could stitch about ⅟₁₆˝ to ⅛˝ from the inside edge, or hand stitch the binding in place.

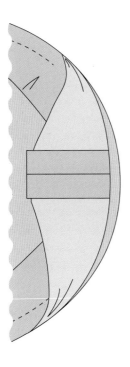

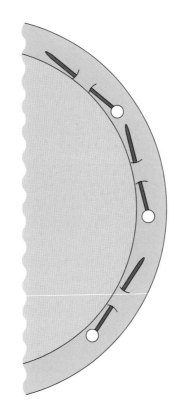

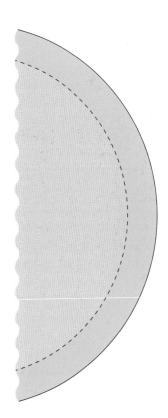

## Piping

Piping adds not only visual appeal and professional details to your projects, but also strength and structure to seams and corners. Make piping by folding bias-cut strips, referring to Double-Layer Bias Binding, Steps 1–3 (page 15), over piping cord that is purchased by the yard in fabric and upholstery shops.

**1.** Cut the bias strips long enough for your pattern requirements and wide enough to fold over your cord and include seam allowances.

**2.** Lay the cording down the center of the wrong side of the bias strip and fold the bias strip over it, aligning the raw edges.

## Tip ⟵

Pin or clip next to the cord to keep it from moving out of the center, or use double-sided tape such as Dritz Washaway Wonder Tape to hold the cord in place.

**3.** Using a long stitch length, a piping foot, or a zipper foot with the needle on the left side, stitch down the length of the strip very close to the cording, yet still allowing space for 2 more rows of stitching between this row and the cording. If necessary, trim the piping seam allowance to match the seam allowance required for your project. *Figure A*

**4.** Pin or use double-sided tape to secure the piping along the edge of the *right side* of your *main* or *exterior* fabric piece. If you are pinning along curves, clip the seam allowance of the piping and fabric, but do not clip through the stitching.

**5.** Stitch the piping down, making sure you are slightly to the left of the previous piping stitching. This will ensure that the first stitching line does not show when the project is finished. *Figure B*

**6.** Place the *lining* or *back* fabric piece over the piping, *right sides together*, and pin together. Flip the unit over so that the stitching side is up. Stitch the 2 fabric pieces together, stitching slightly to the left of the previous stitching line. *Figure C*

**7.** Fold back the main and lining fabric pieces, exposing the piping, and press next to the piping to flatten the seam allowances.

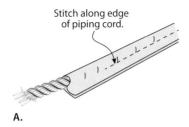

Stitch along edge of piping cord.

**A.**

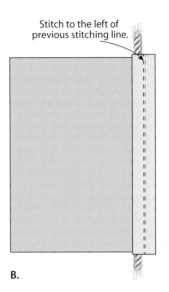

Stitch to the left of previous stitching line.

**B.**

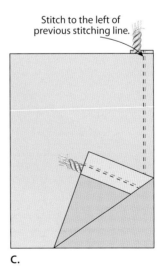

Stitch to the left of previous stitching line.

**C.**

# Hipster
Made by Lindsay Conner
# Pocket Scarf

**Finished size:** 7″ × 33″

*Fabric: Winged by Bonnie Christine, Art Gallery Fabrics*

This infinity-style scarf solves a common problem—what to do with your cash, cards, keys, or cell phone when you have no pockets and don't want to carry a purse. With your ID encased in the secure zippered pocket, you can leave your bulky bag at home! Made with knit rather than cotton fabric, this continuous scarf can be sewn on a sewing machine or serger.

## MATERIALS AND SUPPLIES

- **Jersey knit fabric:** ¾ yard of 58″ wide
- **Zipper:** 7″ length, 1¼″ wide, heavy duty #5
- **Stretch needle for sewing machine**

Use it for:

- Cash and cards
- Cell phone and keys
- Lip balm

# Cutting

**NOTE**

When cutting knit fabrics, it's important to cut along the straight grain so that your fabric hangs nicely and doesn't have any unusual twists. To find the natural grain of your knit, fold it in half crosswise, so the selvages are to the left and the right. Hold the cut raw edges of the fabric and let the bottom fold hang below. Gently shift the folded fabric until it hangs naturally—now you have found the grain. Pin along the fold and cut your pattern pieces accordingly. For example, if cutting a 15″ × width-of-fabric strip, cut 7½″ on each side of the pins.

## Jersey knit fabric:

- Cut 1 piece 15″ × width of fabric for the scarf, making sure to find and cut with the grain.

- Cut 1 piece 9″ × 15″ for the pocket (cutting the 9″ along the width of the fabric, parallel to the previous cut).

- Cut 2 pieces 1½″ × 4″ for the zipper tabs.

# Instructions

*All seam allowances are ½″ unless otherwise noted.*

## Sew the Zippered Pocket

**1.** Fold a zipper tab in half crosswise. Unfold and fold the raw edges in to meet the center line. Repeat with the other zipper tab; each will resemble a mini 4-Fold Open-End Strap (page 10).

**2.** Sandwich the zipper tails on one end of the zipper between the layers of the folded zipper tab. Topstitch ³⁄₁₆″ from the fold through all layers to secure the zipper end inside the tab. Make sure the zipper pull is out of the way when you sew. Repeat with the other end. *Figure A*

**3.** With the *right side* of the zipper facedown on the *right side* of the fabric, align a long edge of the zipper with a 9″ edge of the pocket. Stitch these together using a ¼″ seam allowance. *Figure B*

**4.** Fold the pocket over the seam and press. *Figure C*

**5.** Repeat Steps 3 and 4 to stitch the other edge of the zipper to the other 9″ edge of the pocket, making a fabric loop. *Figure D*

**6.** Topstitch both zipper seams ³⁄₁₆″ from the edge, being careful not to stitch through the back of the pocket. *Figure E*

**A.**

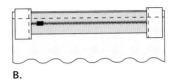

**B.**

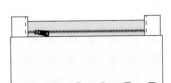

**C.**

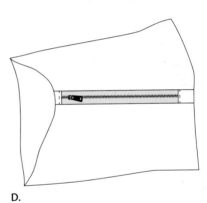

**D.**

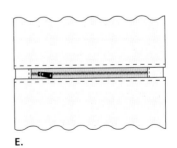

**E.**

## Sew the Scarf

**1.** Fold the scarf in half lengthwise, right sides together, and pin the long raw edges together. Stitch along the seam you've pinned, leaving a 3″ section open in the center for turning. Press the seam of the long tube open.

**2.** With the scarf still turned *wrong side out*, insert the zippered pocket into one open end so that the right sides are together and the raw edges are aligned. The long scarf seam should run opposite the zipper, which is the front of the scarf. Pin the raw edges of the scarf to the pocket, easing the fabric as you go around the loop. *Figure A*

**3.** Stitch the pocket to the scarf by sewing around the loop to join both tubes.

**4.** Reach inside the tube to pull the other side of the pocket toward the other raw edges of the scarf. Align the raw edges, making sure that the scarf is not twisted and that the long scarf seam runs opposite the zipper. Pin the raw edges together and repeat Step 3. *Figure B*

**5.** Reach inside the 3″ opening in the scarf and pull the scarf *right side out*. Position the seams on both ends of the pocket away from the zipper and press along the seams.

**6.** Stitch in-the-ditch along both seams joining the scarf to the pocket. Topstitch ³⁄₁₆″ away from both seams on the scarf side of the pocket. Hand or machine stitch the opening closed. *Figure C*

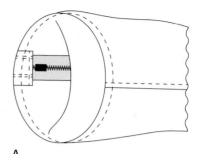

**A.**

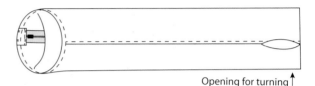

Opening for turning ↑

**B.**

**C.**

**NOTE**

The scarf may be doubled or tripled—either way, your valuables are encased in the roomy pocket and won't slide around in the body of the scarf.

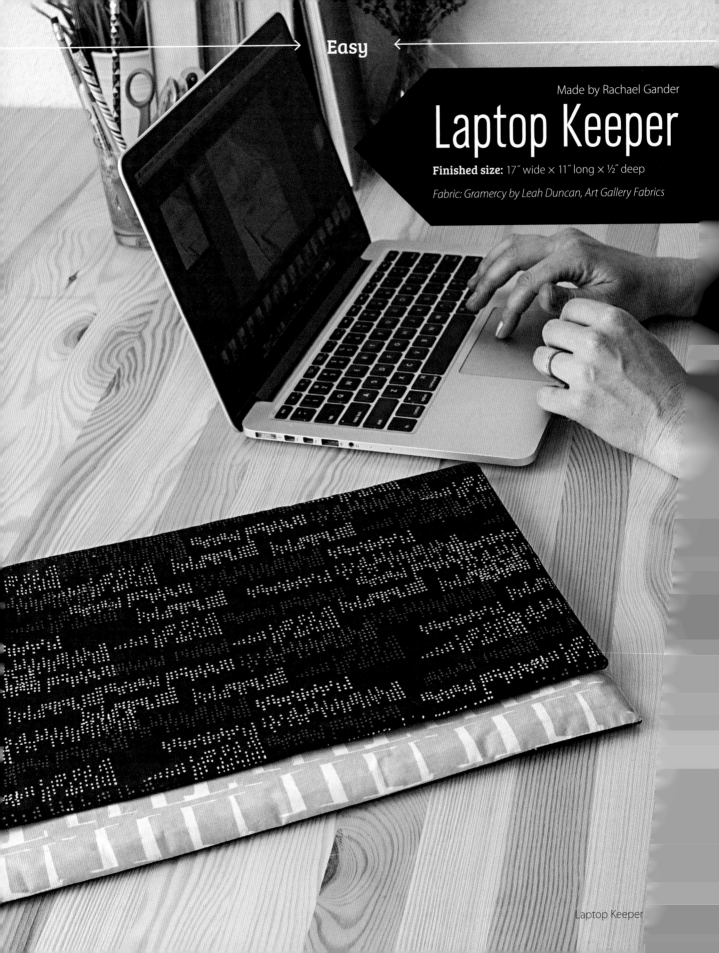

Easy

# Laptop Keeper

**Finished size:** 17″ wide × 11″ long × ½″ deep

*Fabric: Gramercy by Leah Duncan, Art Gallery Fabrics*

Sew a slender laptop cozy to keep precious cargo from scuffs when you're working away from home. A fabric flap with pockets is ideal for stashing business cards or important notes, while an inner zipper houses a plastic sheet to help the folder keep its shape. Stash a charging cord inside, and you're ready for your next meeting.

## MATERIALS AND SUPPLIES

- **Quilting cotton:** 40″-wide quilting cotton

  *Exterior fabric:* ⅝ yard

  *Lining fabric:* ⅝ yard

  *Accent fabric:* ⅜ yard

- **Sew-in fleece:** ½ yard of 45″ wide

- **Interfacing:** 1¼ yards of 20″-wide medium-weight fusible interfacing

- **Template plastic:** 8½″ × 16½″

- **Zipper:** 14″ all-purpose

Use it for:

- Electronics
- Papers and presentations
- Sketchbook and pens
- Business cards and networking tools

# Cutting

## Outer fabric:

- Cut 1 piece 18″ × 22″ for exterior (A).

- Cut 1 piece 18″ × 10″ for small pocket (C).

## Lining fabric:

- Cut 1 piece 18″ × 10″ (E).

- Cut 1 piece 18″ × 13″ (F).

- Cut 1 piece 18″ × 12″ for large pocket lining (B).

## Accent fabric:

- Cut 1 piece 18″ × 12″ for large pocket (D).

## Sew-in fleece:

- Cut 1 piece 16½″ × 20½″ for exterior.

- Cut 1 piece 16½″ × 10½″ for large pocket.

## Interfacing:

- Cut 1 piece 18″ × 22″ for exterior.

- Cut 1 piece 18″ × 12″ for large pocket.

- Cut 1 piece 18″ × 10″ for small pocket.

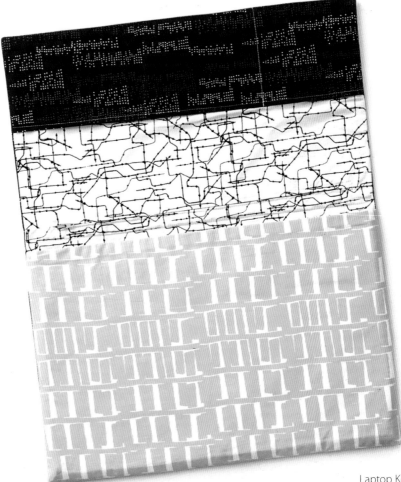

# Instructions

*All seam allowances are ½″. Fuse interfacing per the manufacturer's instructions.*

## Fuse the Interfacing

**1.** Center the larger, 16½″ × 20½″ fleece on the *wrong side* of exterior A. Place the 18″ × 22″ interfacing on top with the fusible side facing down (toward the fleece) and fuse.

**2.** Center the smaller, 16½″ × 10½″ fleece on the *wrong side* of large pocket lining B. Place the 18″ × 12″ interfacing on top with the fusible side facing down (toward the fleece) and fuse.

**3.** Fuse the 18″ × 10″ interfacing to the *wrong side* of small pocket C.

## Insert the Lining Zipper

**1.** Place lining pieces E and F *right sides together*, with the center 18″ edges aligned.

**2.** Starting at one edge and using a ½″ seam allowance, stitch a few stitches, then backstitch. Stitch forward for 2″ and then backstitch. Switch to a long basting stitch and continue basting the seam until 2″ from the end. Switch back to a regular stitch length and stitch a few stitches, backstitch, then continue to finish the seam and backstitch at the end. *Figure A*

**3.** Press the seam allowance open.

**4.** Center the zipper teeth along the seam (*wrong side* of fabric) and pin or tape the zipper in place to hold. *Figure B*

**5.** Using the zipper foot and with the fabric *right side up*, stitch a box around the zipper to secure it to the fabric, removing the pins as needed. *Figure C*

**6.** Use a seam ripper to remove the basting stitches, and test the zipper to make sure that it opens freely.

> **NOTE**
> Leave the zipper open for turning the bag right side out later.

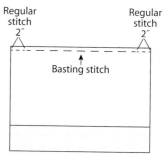

Regular stitch 2″ · Regular stitch 2″ · Basting stitch

**A.**

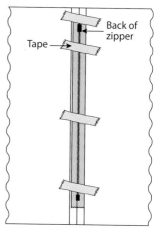

Tape · Back of zipper

**B.**

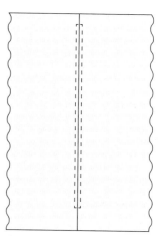

**C.**

## Make the Large Pocket

**1.** Place large pocket pieces B and D *right sides together* and stitch together along one 18″ side. Turn *right sides out*, so the wrong sides are touching, and press the seam. Topstitch ⅛″ from the seam.

**2.** Place the zippered lining piece right side up, with piece F to the right. Pin the large pocket to the right side of lining piece F, aligning raw 18″ edges. The *lining side* of the pocket should face the *right side* of the zippered lining, and the pocket opening should face the zipper. Baste the top, right, and bottom edges together.

## Make the Small Pocket

**1.** Fold small pocket piece C *wrong sides together* so that the 18″ edges align and press well.

**2.** Topstitch ⅛″ from the folded edge.

**3.** Pin pocket (C) to the left side of lining piece E, aligning raw 18″ edges. The *back* of the pocket should face the *right side* of the lining. Baste the top, bottom, and left edges together, leaving the right side (edge with the fold) open.

**4.** Mark 6″ down from the top side of the pocket with tape or chalk pencil.

**5.** Stitch across the pocket to divide into segments as shown, backstitching at both ends to secure. *Figure A*

## Finishing

**1.** Pin the lining and exterior *right sides together*, making sure the zipper is open and lining up the side seams and raw edges. Stitch around the perimeter.

**2.** Clip the corners and turn the folio *right side out* through the zipper opening.

**3.** Stitch a straight line through all layers ¾″ away from the zipper (on the side closer to the large pocket), backstitching at both ends to secure. Fold on this stitched line and press. *Figure B*

**4.** Insert the template plastic into the zippered pocket for stability.

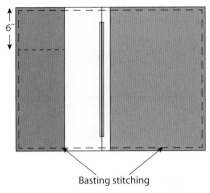

6″

Basting stitching

**A.**

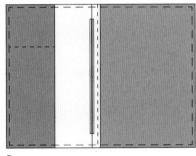

**B.**

Made by Mary Jaracz

# The Man Clutch

**Finished size:**
Open: 10″ wide × 11½″ high
Closed: 10″ × 5¾″

*Fabric: Midweight herringbone wool (exterior), Benzy Skepp, IKEA (interior). Panama Wave in Peachtini, Waverly (exterior), solid canvas (interior).*

Everyone can use a sleek, pocketed clutch to store the basics. Sewn in masculine fabrics, The Man Clutch was designed as a gift for my husband, to store his favorite things, but it also doubles as a stealthy carrier for a diaper and wipes for the parent on the go! A center zippered pocket stores a cell phone or other small items you want to keep secure.

**Use it for:**

- Diaper and wipes
- Journal or sketchbook
- Unisex carryall

## MATERIALS AND SUPPLIES

- **Home decor cotton, canvas, upholstery, or heavyweight fabric:**

  *Fabric A:* ⅓ yard for clutch exterior and zipper pouch lining

  *Fabric B:* ⅓ yard for clutch interior and zipper pouch exterior

- **Zipper:** 9″ (denim zipper with metal teeth)
- **Zipper foot**
- **Roller foot** *(optional)*

### LEATHER ACCENTS (OPTION A):

- **Soft, thin leather:** 4″ × 20″
- **Dritz Washaway Wonder Tape** *(optional):* 20″ of ¼″ wide

### FABRIC ACCENTS (OPTION B):

- **Fabric:** ⅛ yard
- **Canvas or polyester webbing or belting:** 1″ wide × 14″ long
- **Adjustable slider:** 1″

# Cutting

## Fabric A:

- Cut 1 rectangle 11″ × 20″ for the clutch body exterior.

- Cut 2 rectangles 5″ × 10⅜″ for the zipper pouch lining.

## Fabric B:

- Cut 1 rectangle 11″ × 20″ for the clutch interior.

- Cut 2 rectangles 5″ × 10⅜″ for the zipper pouch exterior.

- Cut 2 rectangles 1″ × 2¼″ for the zipper tabs.

## Leather accents (Option A):

- Cut 1 leather rectangle 3½″ × 10¼″.

- Cut 1 leather strip ½″ × 20″.

- Cut 1 leather strip ⅝″ × 2″.

## Fabric accents (Option B):

- Cut 1 rectangle 4¼″ × 11″.

- Cut webbing into 2 pieces 4½″ and 9½″.

# Instructions

*All seam allowances are ⅜″ unless otherwise noted.*

## Make the Clutch

**1.** Place the clutch exterior and interior 11″ × 20″ large rectangles *right sides together*. Sew all 4 sides together with a ⅜″ seam allowance, leaving a 3″ opening on one short side. Clip the corners. *Figure A*

**2.** Turn the rectangle *right side out* and push out the corners. Fold in the edges from the 3″ opening by ⅜″ and press. Topstitch ⅛″ and then ¼″ away from the edge around the entire rectangle. *Figure B*

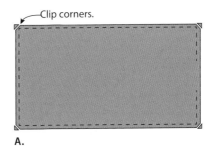

Clip corners.

**A.**

**B.**

## Option A: Leather Accents/Closure

**1.** Place the clutch rectangle horizontally with the *exterior fabric facing up*. Center the 3½″ × 10¼″ leather rectangle vertically. Lay down 2 strips of adhesive tape on either side of the center and press the leather down on top to hold it in place. Trim any excess leather from the top and bottom edges. If desired, change the bobbin thread to match the interior fabric. Using a long stitch length (4 mm or 6 stitches per inch), sew a vertical line down the center of the leather. Then sew around all the outside edges using a ⅛″ seam allowance. If adhesive tape is not available, pins can be used as a guide to mark the location of the leather strip. Just be careful to pin exactly in the seamline, as the pinholes will be permanent. *Figure A*

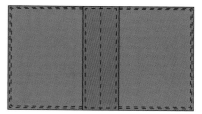

**A.**

- - - - - - - - - - - - - - - - - - - - - - - - - - - - - - - - - - - - - - - -

## Tip ←

**A regular needle and standard presser foot should work with soft, thin leather. However, using a roller foot may help the leather feed more smoothly. If you do not have a roller foot and your regular foot is sticking to the leather, try covering the bottom of your presser foot with a satin-finish tape.**

- - - - - - - - - - - - - - - - - - - - - - - - - - - - - - - - - - - - - - - -

**2.** With the *exterior still facing up*, measure 5¾″ in from the left side and mark. Place the long strip of leather horizontally, centered with the end of the strip at the 5¾″ mark, and place pins over (not through) the leather to secure. Sew the leather end in place with a 1″ × ⅜″ rectangle. Measure 5½″ from the right side and place the left, long edge of the short leather strip vertically and centered. Sew the ends down with either a ⅜″ square or 2 straight lines ⅜″ apart. *Figure B*

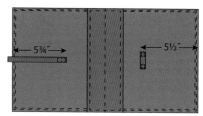

**B.**

## Option B: Fabric Accents/Closure

**1.** Take the accent fabric strip and press each edge ⅜″ to the *wrong side*. Unfold the edges and miter the corners as pictured, then refold and press the 4 edges. *Figure A*

**2.** Pin and sew the fabric strip to the center of the clutch exterior as in Option A, Step 1 (page 34), except using a standard stitch length. *Figure B*

**3.** Prepare the 4½″ and 9½″ strap pieces. If using a synthetic strap, use a match or lighter to slightly melt the cut edges. On the 4½″ piece, fold one end under by 1″ and zigzag stitch back and forth until the raw edges are covered. Loop the other end over the middle bar of the adjustable slider, fold it back 1″, and zigzag stitch down. On the 9½″ piece, fold each end under by 1″ and use a zigzag stitch to secure. *Figure C*

**4.** With the *exterior still facing up*, measure 1″ to either side of the center fabric strip. Center one strap on either side and pin in place. Secure each end by sewing a ¾″ square with an X inside. *Figure D*

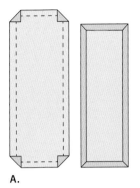

A.

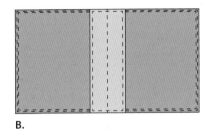

B.

C.

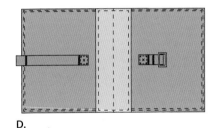

D.

## Side Pockets

With the interior of the clutch facing up, fold over each short end 3¾˝ to form the side pockets. Make sure the top and bottom are flush with the rest of the clutch, even if there is a slight gap in the pocket. To secure the pockets, stitch along the pocket sides over the previous ⅛˝ and ¼˝ topstitching. The outer piece is now complete. Set aside and start working on the zipper pouch. *Figure A*

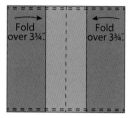

A.

## Zipper Pouch

**1.** Fold the fabric zipper tabs in half crosswise, *wrong sides together*. Center the folded edge of 1 tab just above the zipper head on the top side and pin. Center the other folded square just below the zipper stop and pin. Using a zipper foot, stitch ⅛˝ away from the folded edge. Go slowly to avoid breaking a needle. *Figure B*

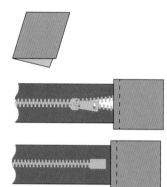

B.

**2.** At the top of the *right side* of one zippered pouch exterior fabric piece, center the zipper with the zipper pull facing down. Stitch ⁵⁄₁₆˝ away from the long top edge using a zipper foot. *Figure C*

C.

**3.** Turn the zipper up and press the seam allowance away from the zipper. With *right sides together* pin the other edge of the zipper to the top edge of the other zippered pouch exterior fabric piece. Stitch ⁵⁄₁₆″ away from the top edge using a zipper foot. Open and press the fabric away from the zipper. *Figure D*

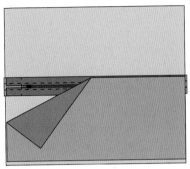

**D.**

**4.** To attach the lining, lay the zippered piece with the fabric *wrong side up*. Place the zippered pouch lining fabric *wrong side up* at the top of the zipper. Sew the lining to the zipper ³⁄₁₆″ away from the edge of the lining fabric. *Figure E*

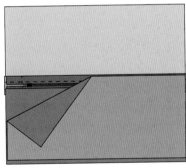

**E**

**5.** Fold back the lining fabric attached in Step 4 so it is now *right side up* against 1 exterior piece and the back of the zipper is visible. Line up the other piece of the lining fabric with the exposed top edge of the zipper and stitch ³⁄₁₆″ from the edge. Open lining panels and press flat. If the zipper tabs stick out, trim them so the sides are flush. *Figure F*

**6.** Make sure the zipper is open. With *right sides together*, line up the 2 exterior pieces with each other, and the 2 lining pieces with each other. Fold the zipper in half lengthwise with the zipper teeth toward the lining fabric. *Figure G*

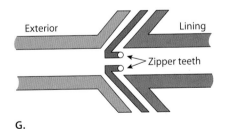

**F.**

Exterior        Lining

Zipper teeth

**G.**

**7.** Sew all the way around the perimeter with a ⅜″ seam allowance, leaving a 4″ opening at the bottom of the lining for turning. Clip the corners and press. *Figure H*

**8.** Through the opening in the bottom of the lining, turn the bag right side out and push out the corners. Hand stitch the opening in the lining closed. Push the lining inside of the exterior and press flat.

**9.** Center the bottom of the zippered pouch on the stitched center line of the clutch interior. Using a small slipstitch, hand stitch the bottom of the zippered pouch to the clutch interior. Sew only through the top layers of fabric and not through the outer leather or fabric strip. *Figure I*

> ### NOTE
> To close the leather option, wrap the long leather strap all the way around once, then tuck it under the short piece. The leather strap will keep the clutch closed. For a more secure closure, use the canvas/belting strap and adjustable slider option.

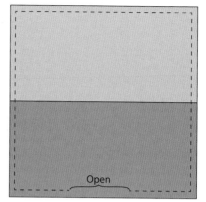

H.

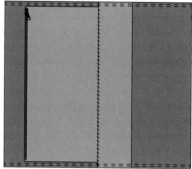

I.

Made by Michelle Webster

# Handy Purse Pockets

**Finished size:** 22″ × 5¾″ (not including tab)

*Fabric: Vera's Garden, Robert Kaufman*

What's better than having a bag with lots of pockets? How about pockets you can quickly swap from bag to bag? This wrap-around purse organizer has a special feature that helps it to stand up and keep its shape inside any standard purse, and the slip pockets and gusseted pocket on both the inside and outside of the loop make it twice as handy. Don't leave your favorite pen in your "other purse" again!

**Use it for:**

- Purse contents
- Wallet and keys
- Makeup

## MATERIALS AND SUPPLIES

- **Quilting cotton:** 44″ wide

  *Outer fabric:* ¾ yard

  *Lining fabric:* ⅜ yard

- **Interfacing:** 1⅜ yard of 20″-wide light- to medium-weight, woven, fusible interfacing (such as Pellon Shape-Flex SF101 or Handler Form-Flex All Purpose)

- **Sew-on hook-and-loop tape:** ¾″ wide, 3″ length

### NOTE

Fabric amounts are based on cutting the exterior and lining fabrics with the shorter edges following the lengthwise grain, and the interfacing pieces with the longer edges following the lengthwise grain. Since most interfacing is only 20″ wide, you'll need the amount indicated to cut full pieces. You can also cut 2 pieces of interfacing to make the equivalent of the dimensions shown in the cutting diagrams, and then patch them together by slightly overlapping the edges when fusing the interfacing in place. You'll need 1 yard of 20″-wide interfacing if you are patching the pieces. You may omit the interfacing if you choose a heavier-weight fabric.

# Cutting

## Outer fabrics:

- Cut 2 pieces 23˝ × 6½˝ for main panel (A).

- Cut 1 piece 23˝ × 5¼˝ for pockets (B).

- Cut 1 piece 25˝ × 5¾˝ for pockets (C).

## Lining fabrics:

- Cut 1 piece 23˝ × 5¼˝ for pockets (B).

- Cut 1 piece 25˝ × 5¾˝ for pockets (C).

- Cut 1 piece 3˝ × 4˝ for tab (D).

## Interfacing:

- Cut 2 pieces 22½˝ × 6¼˝ for main panel (A).

- Cut 1 piece 22½˝ × 5˝ for pockets (B).

- Cut 1 piece 24½˝ × 5½˝ for pockets (C).

- Cut 1 piece 2¾˝ × 3¾˝ for tab (D).

# Instructions

*All seam allowances are ¼″ unless otherwise noted.*

## Trim Corners Off Interfacing and Fuse to Fabrics

**1.** Stack interfacing A pieces on top of each other and then fold the pieces side to side. Cutting through all layers at once, trim away a ¾″ square from the top and bottom corners.

**2.** Fold interfacing D in half from side to side and then top to bottom. Cutting through all layers at once, trim away a ¾″ square from the unfolded corner.

**3.** Center and fuse interfacing A, B, and C to corresponding exterior pieces A, B, and C. Fuse interfacing D to lining D.

## Make the Panels B and C

**1.** Place lining B and exterior B *right sides together* and sew them together along one long edge. Do the same with lining C and exterior C.

**2.** Press the seams open, fold the pieces away from each other so they are *wrong sides together*, and press the top seams of both B and C.

**3.** Topstitch along the seams at ⅛″ and ¼″. The extra row of topstitching is optional, but it will add some additional stability to the pocket openings.

> **NOTE**
>
> The purpose of trimming the interfacing is to remove some bulk and make sewing easier. The trimming doesn't need to be exact—just remove about the amount indicated. All interfacing pieces are applied to the *wrong side* of fabric pieces.

## Assemble the Pocket Panel C

**1.** With the C panel *right side up*, measure from the left side and mark the top and bottom at 6″, 7″, 9″, and 10″.

**2.** At the 7″ mark, fold C so that the lining fabrics are now *right sides together*.

**3.** Beginning from the bottom of C, edgestitch the folded edge. *Figure A*

**4.** Unfold the fabric and then refold it again at the 9″ mark.

**5.** Beginning at the bottom of C, edgestitch the folded edge. *Figure B*

**6.** With the panel right side up, match the fold at 7″ to the 6″ marks and pin at the bottom.

**7.** Match the fold at 9″ to the 10″ marks and pin at the bottom.

**8.** Baste the folds in place along the bottom of C. *Figure C*

**9.** With *right sides up*, place C over one A piece, aligning the bottom and side edges. Baste C to A around the sides and bottom. *Figure D*

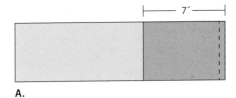

**A.**

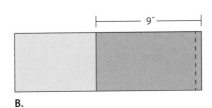

**B.**

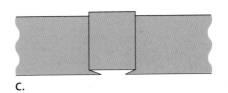

**C.**

**D.**

## Make the Closure Tab

**1.** With *wrong sides together*, fold D in half along the 4˝ sides, and press to crease the center, then unfold.

**2.** On the right side of the fabric, center the hook half of the hook-and-loop tape about ¼˝ below the center crease and sew around the perimeter of the tape ⅛˝ from the edge to secure. *Figure A*

**3.** Fold D in half along the crease with *right sides together.*

**4.** Stitch together D along the 2 short ends.

**5.** Clip the corners at the folded edge. *Figure B*

**6.** Turn D *right side* out.

**7.** Edgestitch along the sewn and folded edges.

## Assemble Pocket Panel B

**1.** Place pocket panel B exterior side up. Place the closure tab on the right short edge so that the hook tape faces up and is about ⅛˝ below the top of B. Baste the closure tab to B.

**2.** Along the left side of B, align the loop half of the hook-and-loop tape ½˝ below the top and ¾˝ from the left short edge of B. Sew around the perimeter of the tape ⅛˝ from the edge to secure. *Figure C*

**3.** Place B *right side up* on the remaining A piece.

**4.** Measuring from the left edge of B, mark lines for the pen slips at 5˝, 6˝, 7˝, 8˝, and 9˝.

**5.** Sew the pen slips by stitching directly on the lines marked in the previous step. Backstitch well where B meets A. *Figure D*

**6.** Baste B to A around the sides and bottom.

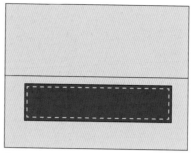

A.

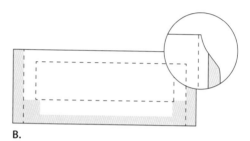

B.

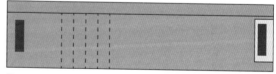

C.

D.

## Assemble Front and Back

**1.** Place A/B and A/C pieces *right sides together*. Sew around the outside perimeter, leaving a 5″ opening along the center top of A. *Figure E*

**2.** Clip all 4 corners. Turn the piece *right side* out through the opening. Push all corners out neatly and press.

**3.** Slipstitch the opening closed.

**4.** Topstitch across the top edge of A.

## Make the Pocket Dividers

**1.** With the C side facing *right side up*, measure from the left edge and mark at 4½″ and 8½″. Beginning from the bottom of C, stitch the vertical pocket divisions at the 4½″ and 8½″ marks. *Figure F*

**2.** With the B side facing *right side up*, and beginning from the bottom of B, stitch directly over or right next to the 2 rows of stitching at the outer edges of the pen slips (approximately 4½″ and 8½″). Trim away any stray threads, and you're done! *Figure G*

E.

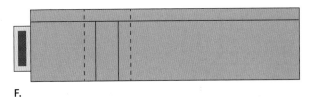

F.

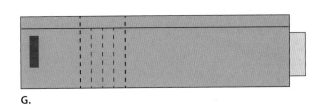

G.

Made by Samantha Hussey

# Padded Bag Insert

**Finished size:** 14˝ wide × 5¼˝ tall × 4¾˝ deep

Watch the magic happen when you add this padded interior to turn your bag into the perfect camera bag. Store your DSLR and extra lenses in this cozy, divided bag insert.

## MATERIALS AND SUPPLIES

- **Quilting cotton to match your bag lining:** ⅞ yard
- **Foam:** ½˝ thick, 24˝ wide, ½ yard
- **Hook-and-loop tape:** ¾˝ wide, 2½ yards

Use it for:

- Camera and lenses
- Baby gear

# Cutting

## Cotton fabric:

- Cut 3 rectangles 11″ × 15″ for fabric base and sides.

- Cut 2 rectangles 6″ × 11″ for fabric ends.

- Cut 1 rectangle 6″ × 10½″ for each fabric divider.

## Foam:

- Cut 1 rectangle 5″ × 14″ for foam base.

- Cut 2 rectangles 4½″ × 14″ for foam sides.

- Cut 2 rectangles 4½″ × 3¼″ for foam ends.

- Cut 1 rectangle 4″ × 3¼″ for each foam divider.

## Hook-and-loop tape:

- Cut 2 strips 14″ long of soft loop tape for base.

- Cut 4 strips 12″ long of soft loop tape for sides.

- Cut 2 strips 12″ long of hard hook tape for sides.

- Cut 4 strips 4½″ long of hard hook tape for ends.

- Cut 2 strips 4″ long of hard hook tape for each divider.

# Instructions

*All seam allowances are ¼˝ unless otherwise noted.*

## Make the Base

**1.** With the fabric base *right side up*, place a base strip of soft loop tape along one long edge, keeping the top edge of the loop tape ¾˝ from the edge of the fabric and the strip centered between the short edges. The top edge of the second strip will be 4¼˝ below the top edge of the fabric. Pin as needed and stitch these in place. *Figure A*

**2.** Fold the fabric base in half lengthwise, enclosing the loop tape, and pin.

**3.** Stitch around 3 open sides, leaving a large opening for turning in the center bottom edge. Backstitch at the start and stop. Baste the opening closed. *Figure B*

**4.** Press to set the basting stitches and then unpick between the backstitching.

**5.** Box all 4 corners to a ½˝ width by folding each corner flat with the seam centered. Mark and stitch a line ½˝ long across the point. *Figure C*

**6.** Turn right sides out and insert foam base.

**7.** Pin the opening closed and stitch using an invisible slip stitch. *Figure D*

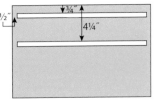

A.

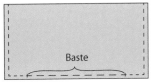

B.

C.

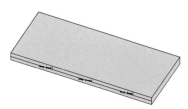

D.

## Make the Sides

**1.** With the fabric side *right side up*, place a side strip of soft loop tape along one long edge, keeping the top edge of the loop tape 1″ from the edge of the fabric and the strip centered between the short edges. Position and stick the second loop strip 3″ from the top. Position and stick the strip of hard hook tape 5″ from the top. Stitch these in place. *Figure A*

**2.** Repeat Step 1 for the second fabric side.

**3.** Fold each of the fabric sides in half lengthwise, enclosing the loop tape, and pin.

**4.** Repeat Make the Base, Steps 3–7 (page 49), completing both sides.

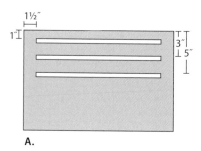

A.

B.

## Make the Ends

**1.** Fold an end piece in half crosswise with *right sides together* and pin.

**2.** Stitch around 3 open sides, leaving a large opening for turning on the end. Backstitch at the start and stop. Baste the opening closed. *Figure B*

**3.** Press to set the basting stitches and then unpick between the backstitching.

**4.** Clip corners and then turn it right sides out

**5.** Center a strip of the hard hook tape between the folded end and the open end. Stitch in place. Repeat for the other side. *Figure C*

**6.** Insert foam, pushing it right into the corners.

**7.** Pin the opening for turning closed, matching basting stitch holes, and then stitch the opening closed. *Figure D*

**8.** Repeat to make the other end.

C.

D.

## Make the Dividers

Construct the dividers in the same manner as the ends, for as many dividers as you desire.

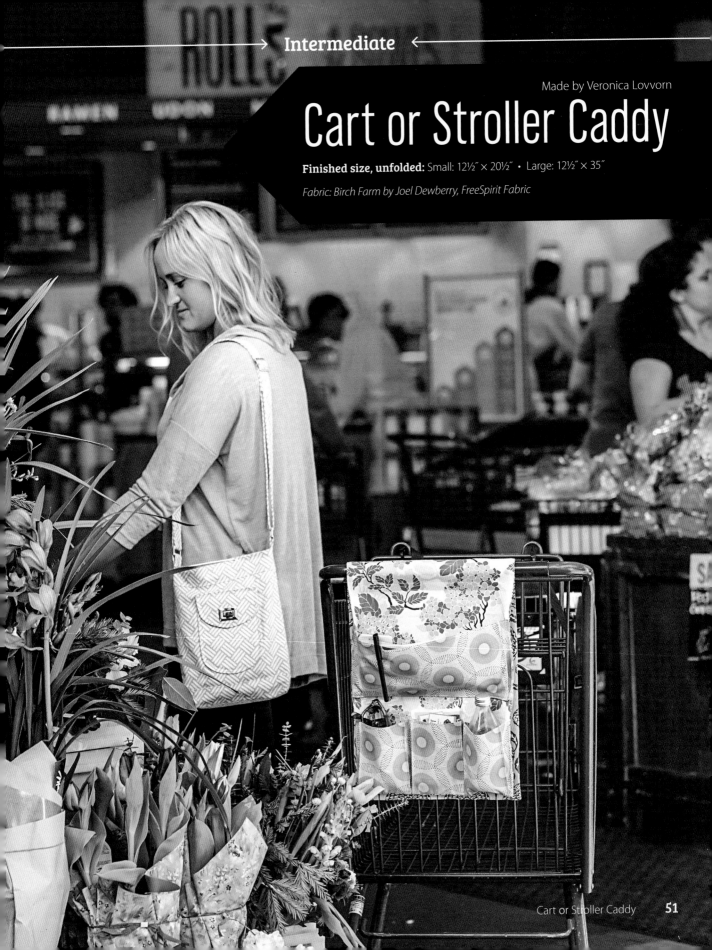

Made by Veronica Lovvorn

# Cart or Stroller Caddy

**Finished size, unfolded:** Small: 12½˝ × 20½˝  •  Large: 12½˝ × 35˝

*Fabric: Birch Farm by Joel Dewberry, FreeSpirit Fabric*

These pockets that go with you to the grocery store keep your cart organized, from coupons to a shopping list and everything else you need to keep at arm's length. Make the portable pockets in two different sizes and mix and match the pocket options to customize according to what you carry the most. This easy hook-on accessory fits the handle of a baby stroller too, so you won't have to reach into a bottomless pit for a bottle.

## Use it for:

- Grocery list and coupons
- Child's snacks and toys
- Hand wipes

## MATERIALS AND SUPPLIES

- **Quilting cotton:**

  *For small organizer:* ⅞ yard

  *For large organizer:* 1⅝ yards

- **Interfacing:** 20″-wide light- to medium-weight woven fusible interfacing (such as Pellon Shape-Flex SF101)

  *For small organizer:* 1⅛ yards

  *For large organizer:* 1½ yards

- **Water-soluble fabric marker**
- **Ruler**
- **Point turner**
- **Sew-on hook-and-loop tape:** ¾″ wide, 11″ length
- **Dritz Washaway Wonder Tape** *(optional)*

# Cutting

## Fabric

- **Small:** Cut 2 rectangles 13″ × 21″ for front and back.

- **Large:** Cut 4 rectangles 13″ × 18″ for front and back.

*Choose 2 pockets for a small organizer and 4 pockets for a large organizer:*

- Cut 1 rectangle 19″ × 12″ for pocket A (3 pockets).

- Cut 1 rectangle 17″ × 12″ for pocket B (2 pockets).

- Cut 1 rectangle 17″ × 12″ for pocket C (2 off-centered pockets).

- Cut 1 rectangle 15″ × 12″ for pocket D (1 pocket).

## Interfacing

- **Small:** Cut 1 rectangle 13″ × 21″ for front.

- **Large:** Cut 2 rectangles 13″ × 18″ for front.

*Choose 2 pockets for a small organizer and 4 pockets for a large organizer:*

- Cut 1 rectangle 19″ × 6″ for pocket A.

- Cut 1 rectangle 17″ × 6″ for pocket B.

- Cut 1 rectangle 17″ × 6″ for pocket C.

- Cut 1 rectangle 15″ × 6″ for pocket D.

# Instructions

*All seam allowances are ¼".*

## Pick a Size and Pocket Combination

**1.** Choose to make the small or the large version of the organizer.

**2.** Pick 2 pockets for a small organizer and pick 4 pockets for a large organizer.

## Make the Pockets

**1.** Fold the pocket in half lengthwise with wrong sides together. Press.

**2.** Open the pocket with the wrong side facing up. Fuse the interfacing, according to the manufacturer's directions, to the top half of the wrong side of the pocket.

**3.** Follow these instructions for the small or large organizer:

- *For small organizer pockets and large organizer bottom-level pockets (those placed at lower edge):* Fold the pocket in half wrong sides together along the same fold line and press.

- *For large organizer top-level pockets only (those placed above bottom-level pockets):* Fold the pocket in half with right sides together. Sew together along the long edge only and then turn the pocket right side out. Press.

**4.** Place the interfaced side of the pocket right side up with the folded edge at the top.

**5.** Stitch along the top fold line ⅛" away from the fabric edge.

**6.** Measure from the left edge of the pocket and use a water-soluble fabric marker to draw the dashed or solid pleat lines (*Figure A*) at the specified locations for each pocket A, B, C, and D (see Line Placement chart, page 55).

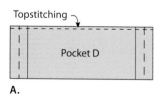

Topstitching

Pocket D

**A.**

## Line Placement

| | Dashed | Solid | Solid | Dashed | Solid | Solid | Dashed | Solid | Solid | Dashed |
|---|---|---|---|---|---|---|---|---|---|---|
| **A** | ½″ | 1½″ | 5½″ | 6½″ | 7½″ | 11½″ | 12½″ | 13½″ | 17½″ | 18½″ |
| **B** | ½″ | 1½″ | 7½″ | 8½″ | 9½″ | 15½″ | 16½″ | | | |
| **C** | ½″ | 1½″ | 9½″ | 10½″ | 11½″ | 15½″ | 16½″ | | | |
| **D** | ½″ | 1½″ | 13½″ | 14½″ | | | | | | |

**7.** Create each pleat by folding along the solid line so the back sides of the pocket are facing. Press and stitch ⅛″ away from each fold. *Figure B*

**8.** Fold each pleat over to the dashed line near the edge. Press thoroughly. *Figure C*

**9.** Pin the folds in place. *Figure D*

**10.** Repeat Steps 1–9 for additional pockets.

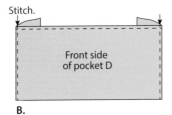

Stitch.

Front side of pocket D

**B.**

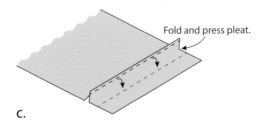

Fold and press pleat.

**C.**

Pleated          Pleated

**D.**

## Small Organizer Assembly

**1.** Fuse interfacing to the wrong side of the front.

**2.** Place the front right side up.

**3.** Center a pocket front side up on each short end of the front. Match the bottom raw edge of the pocket to the short raw edge of the front. Pin in place.

**4.** Stitch each pocket in place by sewing along the dashed lines you marked earlier. Sew the 2 outermost markings first and then sew along the interior markings (if applicable). Baste the pleats closed within the bottom seam allowance.

**5.** Place the back on top of the front with right sides together. Pin.

**6.** Starting ½″ above a pocket, sew around the perimeter of the organizer. Stop ½″ above the opposite pocket, leaving a 4″ opening for turning. Backstitch at the start and stop.

**7.** Clip the corners and turn the organizer right side out through the opening.

**8.** Use a point turner to gently push out the corners of the organizer.

**9.** Turn under the raw edges of the opening and press the organizer thoroughly. Pin the opening closed. *Figure A*

**10.** Topstitch ⅛″ from both edges of the organizer between the 2 pockets, sewing the opening closed.

**11.** Fold the organizer in half with the front sides together. On the back of the organizer, use a water-soluble fabric marker to mark the center on each end of the fold. *Figure B*

**12.** Measure 2″ to the left and right of the center and make a mark. Repeat for the opposite edge of the organizer.

**13.** Use a ruler and a water-soluble fabric marker to connect the marks on the opposite sides and draw 2 lines across the back.

**14.** Separate the 2 sides of the hook-and-loop tape. *Figure C*

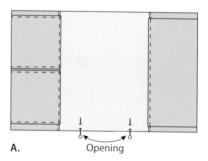

**A.** Opening

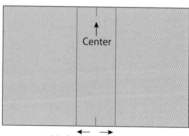

Center

**B.** Mark placement lines 2″ from center.

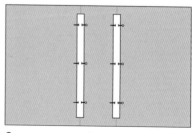

**C.**

**15.** Center and place the top edge of the hook-and-loop tape at the lines drawn in Step 13. Use Wonder Tape or pins to temporarily secure the hook-and-loop tape in place.

**16.** Sew each strip of hook-and-loop tape in place by sewing around all 4 edges. Use thread the color of the hook-and-loop tape on top and thread that matches the fabric in the bobbin.

## Large Organizer Assembly

**1.** Fuse interfacing to the wrong side of both front pieces.

**2.** Place the front pieces right sides together and sew along the top. Repeat for the back pieces. Press the seams open.

**3.** Place the front right side up.

**4.** Center a bottom pocket front side up on each short end of the front. Match the bottom raw edge of the pocket to the short raw edge of the front. Pin in place.

**5.** Stitch each pocket in place by sewing along the dashed lines you marked earlier. Start by sewing the 2 outermost markings first and then sew along the interior markings. Baste the pleats closed within the bottom seam allowance. *Figure A*

**6.** From the top of each bottom pocket end, measure up 1½″ and mark using a water-soluble fabric marker.

**7.** Use a ruler to line up the markings and draw a straight line across the organizer. *Figure B*

**8.** Center a top pocket front side up along each of these lines and pin. *Figure C*

**9.** Stitch each top pocket in place by sewing along the dashed lines you marked earlier. Start by sewing the 2 outermost markings first and then sew along the interior markings.

**10.** Sew ⅛″ from the bottom edge of each top pocket to secure it to the organizer front.

**11.** Place the back on top of the front with right sides together. Match the center seam and pin around the edges.

**12.** Starting ½″ above a top pocket, sew around the perimeter of the organizer. Stop ½″ above the opposite pocket, leaving a 6″ opening for turning. Backstitch at the start and stop.

**13.** Follow the instructions under Small Organizer Assembly, Steps 7–16 (page 56).

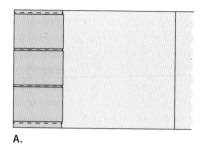

A.

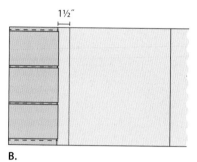

B.

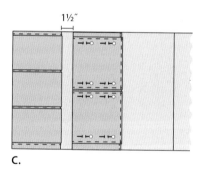

C.

Made by Janelle MacKay

# Park Blanket

**Finished size:**
Blanket: 53″ × 53″
Folded into carrying bag: 11″ × 14″ × 4″

*Fabric: Ribbon Cuddle in Cherry from Shannon Fabrics,*
*Urban Zoologie by Ann Kelle for Robert Kaufman*

Enjoying the great outdoors is always better when you come prepared. Keep this handy picnic blanket in the car so that you can roll it out at a moment's notice. It folds up into a tote, so you can toss it over your shoulder and take it with you anywhere. The laminate on the back will protect you from wet grass and can easily be wiped clean.

**Use it for:**

• Picnics

• Going to the park

• Sporting events

• Outdoor concerts

## PATTERN PIECES

*Refer to Pattern Pieces (page 6).*

• Corner (pattern pullout page P2) (*Refer to Curved Corners, page 7.*)

## MATERIALS AND SUPPLIES

• **Minky fabric:** 1½ yards of 60″ wide

• **Laminated cotton:** 2 yards of 58″ wide

• **Batting:** 53″ × 53″, plus an additional scrap 11″ × 11″

• **Double-fold bias tape:** ½″ wide, 1 yard

• **Sew-on hook-and-loop tape:** 6″ length

• **Walking foot or Teflon presser foot**

• **Spray adhesive for quilting**

• **Paper clips, binder clips, or Clover Wonder clips**

# Cutting

## Minky fabric:

- Cut 1 piece 51″ × 51″ for top.

## Laminated cotton:

- Cut 1 piece 57″ × 57″ for backing.

- Cut 2 pieces 11″ × 11″ for flap.

- Cut 1 strip 6″ × 34½″ for strap.

# Instructions

*All seam allowances are ⅜″ unless otherwise noted. (In this project, ¼″ seam allowances are used for basting pieces in place.)*

## Make the Blanket

**Make the Flap**

**1.** Use the 5¼″ marking on the corner template to mark and cut off 2 curved corners on the bottom edge of one of the flap pieces.

**2.** Using this piece as your template, trace and cut off the corners on the second flap piece and the 11″ × 11″ batting piece.

**3.** On top of the 11″ × 11″ batting piece, place one of the flap pieces *right side up*. Pin or clip the layers together and baste around all 4 sides, using a ¼″ seam allowance. *Figure A*

**4.** On the laminated cotton side of this flap piece, place the 6″ piece of hook tape 1½″ from the edge with the curved corners. Stitch around all 4 sides to secure. *Figure B*

A.

B.

**5.** Place the other flap piece *wrong side* toward the batting, sandwiching the batting between the laminated cotton, which is visible on both sides. Pin or clip the fabric in place and baste around all 4 sides.

**6.** Working on the side of the flap that does not have the hook tape attached, open the folds of the double-fold bias tape and pin or clip it, *right side down*, around the 2 side edges and bottom curved edge. *Figure C*

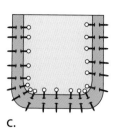

C.

**7.** Stitch along the first fold line of the double-fold bias tape.

**8.** Refold the bias tape along the fold lines around to the back of the flap. Stitch the binding in place by stitching in-the-ditch between the binding and the flap fabric, catching the binding edge on the back side.

### Make and Attach the Strap

**1.** Refer to 4-Fold Open-End Strap (page 10) to create 1 long strap from the strap piece.

**Hint** ▶ When sewing on laminated cotton, you will need to make a few adjustments to accommodate the unique features of the fabric. You may find yourself in a slightly sticky situation, with your presser foot grabbing onto the vinyl surface and not moving along nicely. Switching to a Teflon-coated foot, a roller presser foot, or a walking foot will help you get on your merry way. You can also try slipping a sheet of waxed paper or baker's parchment paper between the laminate and the presser foot. When sewing on laminated cotton, it is also helpful to use a longer stitch length than normal, a new 80/20 needle, and clips or double-sided tape instead of pins. While basting, you may also wish to gently tug the materials from behind the sewing machine, helping to feed them through. With all layers securely pinned or clipped together, your materials shouldn't stretch.

D.

**2.** Pin or clip the ends of the strap to the edge of the flap that does not have bias tape. Position it so that the ends are 1″ from the side edges and baste in place using a ¼″ seam allowance. *Figure D*

### Prepare the Top

**1.** Center the minky top piece, right side up, over the batting piece, measuring from corner to corner to make sure it is square, and being very careful not to stretch it out of shape. *Figure E*

**2.** Pull back the minky, one side at a time, and use quilter's basting spray to adhere the top to the batting. Pin around the outside edges to keep the top in place.

**3.** Using a ¼˝ seam allowance, your walking foot, and a long stitch length, baste around all 4 outside edges. Trim the batting even with the edges of the minky.

**4.** On the batting side, measure and mark ⅜˝ from each corner. These will be your starting and stopping lines for stitching. *Figure F*

### Attach the Flap

With *right sides up* (and hook tape facing down), center the flap on one side of the blanket top, matching raw edges. Clip in place and baste to secure, using a ¼˝ seam allowance. *Figure G*

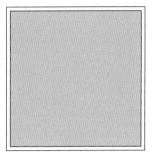

**E.**

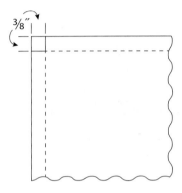

**F.**

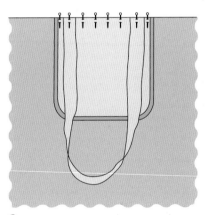

**G.**

## Assemble the Top and Backing

**1.** Fold both the top and backing, marking the centers on the *wrong sides*, on all 4 edges of each.

**2.** With *right sides together*, match the center marks on each side edge of the top and backing. Clip together from the center, joining the top and backing along the raw edges. Because the top is smaller, you should have 3″ of laminated cotton folded beyond the edges of the top. The flap will be inside. *Figure A*

> **NOTE**
>
> The nap of the minky should face downward when lining it up with the laminated cotton (the top of which has the flap). To find the nap, run your hand over the minky and note which direction feels smoother.

**3.** Using a ⅜″ seam allowance and a walking foot, sew along the edge using the ⅜″ marks as your starting and stopping points. Make sure to backstitch at each start and stop.

**4.** Repeat Step 3 to attach the other 3 sides of the top to the backing, making sure to leave a 10″ opening for turning along one side. *Do not turn right side out yet.*

## Make the Mitered Corners

**1.** With the laminated cotton on the back and the batting on the top, fold the blanket diagonally, from corner to corner batting sides together. Match the raw edges of 2 sides, and let your unstitched corners poke out.

**2.** Use a ruler to draw a line from the stitching start/stop point to the diagonal fold you have just made. The line should be 90° with the fold and 45° with the outside edges. *Figure B*

**3.** Sew directly on the marked line, starting at the start/stop stitching line and sewing to the fold. Trim off the corner point, leaving a ¼″ seam allowance. Repeat this on the other 4 corners of the blanket.

**4.** Gently reach through the turning hole and pull the right side of the blanket out. Carefully poke out the corners so they are neat and flat.

3″  Start/stop.

**A.**

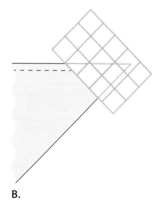

**B.**

## Finishing

**1.** Lay the blanket on a large, flat surface and center the top of the blanket over the backing. The excess backing will fold over to the top and create a frame.

**2.** Measure the frame so that it is straight and even, pinning in-the-ditch between the top and bottom as you go. As you pin, you may need to manipulate the seam allowance so that it faces towards the frame. When you reach the opening for turning, turn the seam allowance under ⅜″ and pin it closed. Hand stitch the hole closed, or stitch it closed with your machine in the next step. *Figure C*

**3.** Using your walking foot and a longer stitch than normal, stitch in-the-ditch between the frame and blanket top.

**4.** Use a pressing cloth and a dry iron on a low/cool setting to press the frame flat.

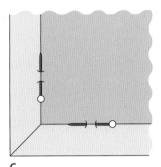

C.

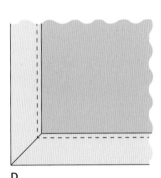

D.

> **NOTE**
>
> To be sure you won't melt the laminated cotton, try this on a test piece first.

**5.** Topstitch around the frame once more, stitching ¼″ from the stitching line you just completed. *Figure D*

**6.** Working from the back of the blanket, flip out and extend the flap past the blanket so that it is open. Pin or clip the frame down onto the flap piece. Staying ¼″ away from the outer frame edge, sew a ¼″-wide box through all the layers to anchor the frame to the flap. *Figure E*

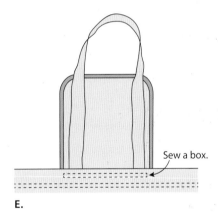

Sew a box.

E.

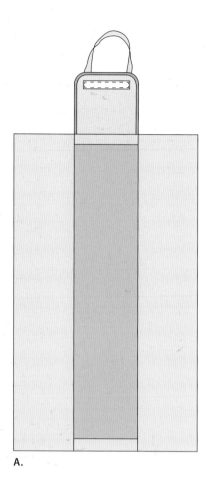

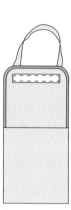

A.                            B.             C.            D.

## Fold into a Carry Bag

**1.** Fold the left and right sides toward the middle of the blanket, meeting them up with the side edges of the flap. *Figure A*

**2.** Fold again, overlapping these sides in the middle section. *Figure B*

**3.** Fold the bottom edge up to meet the top of the blanket. *Figure C*

**4.** Fold the bottom edge up again. *Figure D*

**5.** Fold the flap down and mark the placement spot for the loop side of the hook-and-loop tape. Unfold the blanket and place the loop tape at the marked spot. Stitch the loop tape in place through all layers and around all 4 sides to secure.

Made by Lindsay Conner

# Travel Toiletry Organizer

**Finished size:** Open: 11½˝ × 23½˝ • Closed: 11½˝ × 7¾˝ × ¾˝

*Fabric: Urban Zoologie and Remix by Ann Kelle for Robert Kaufman Fabrics;
Square Elements by Art Gallery Fabrics, Cameron Aquarius Slub by Premier Prints*

One organizer I always take with me on weekend trips is a grab-and-go toiletry roll. The mesh pocket is perfect for airing out items that get wet in the shower, and two zippered pockets keep your makeup and all the other necessities dry. The elastic strap keeps everything wrapped and tidy and also doubles as a hanger for the hotel bathroom door. It works great with a waterproof lining fabric like laminated cotton, but you can also be creative and use materials from around your house (a shower curtain lining and mesh laundry bag, for instance).

**Use it for:**

- Toiletries
- First-aid supplies
- Wet/dry diaper supplies

## PATTERN PIECES

*Refer to Pattern Pieces (page 6).*

- Corner (pattern pullout page P2) *(Refer to Curved Corners, page 7.)*

## MATERIALS AND SUPPLIES

- **Outer and binding fabric:** ¾ yard

- **Lining fabric:** ⅜ yard of a fabric you don't mind getting wet, such as laminated cotton, quilting cotton paired with a pressure-sensitive vinyl coating product (such as Pellon Vinyl Fuse), or oilcloth

- **Bottom pocket fabric:** ⅜ yard if using directional print, ¼ yard if nondirectional

- **Interfacing:** 1⅜ yards of 20˝-wide light- to medium-weight, fusible interfacing (such as Pellon Shape-Flex SF101 or Pellon Fusible Featherweight 911FF)

- **Stabilizer:** 1 package (15˝ × 36˝) of medium-weight fusible stabilizer (such as Pellon Fuse-N-Shape)

- **Zippers:** 2, 9˝ length, all-purpose

- **Regular elastic:** ½˝ wide, 18˝ length

- **Fold-over elastic:** 1˝ wide or ½˝ folded, 12˝ length

- **Mesh:** 8˝ × 16˝ for pocket

# Cutting

## Outer fabric:

- Cut 1 piece 11½″ × 23½″ for main panel.

- Cut 2 or 3 strips on the bias 3″ wide. (See Double-Layer Bias Binding, page 15. You will need about 74″ of finished bias binding.)

## Lining fabrics:

- Cut 1 piece 11½″ × 23½″ for main panel.

- Cut 1 piece 11½″ × 8″ for bottom pocket.

- Cut 2 pieces 11½″ × 4½″ for top pocket.

## Bottom pocket fabric:

- Cut 1 piece 11½″ × 8″ for bottom pocket.

- Cut 4 pieces 11½″ × 3″ for zipper and pocket facings.

- Cut 4 pieces 1½″ × 2½″ for zipper tabs.

## Interfacing:

- Cut 2 pieces 11½″ × 23½″ for outer and lining main panels.

- Cut 1 piece 11½″ × 8″ for bottom pocket.

- Cut 1 piece 11½″ × 4½″ for top pocket.

## Stabilizer:

- Cut 1 piece 11½″ × 23½″ for main panel.

# Instructions

*All seam allowances are ¼″ unless otherwise noted.*

## Fuse the Interfacing and Stabilizer

**1.** Follow the manufacturer's directions to fuse interfacing to the *wrong side* of the main panels of the outer fabric and lining fabric. Fuse interfacing to the *wrong side* of one bottom pocket piece and one lining top pocket piece.

**2.** Follow the manufacturer's directions to fuse stabilizer to the *wrong side* of the main panel cut from lining fabric.

## Prepare the Fabric

**1.** Place the main panel of outer fabric *right side down* with the long edges horizontal. On top, place the main panel of lining fabric (with stabilizer fused to the back) *right side up*.

**2.** Measuring from the left short end of the lining main panel, mark the following measurements across the panel: 2″, 7½″, 14¾″, 17½″. These will be the placement marks for your zippers and facings. *Figure A*

**3.** Round all 4 corners of the main panels using the 3″ marking on the corner template, and then separate the outer and lining fabric.

## Make the Bottom Zipper Pocket

**1.** Use the zipper insertion method in The Man Clutch, Zipper Pouch (page 36), to attach one side of the zipper to the bottom pocket fabric and then the lining of the bottom pocket, leaving the other long side of the zipper unstitched. *Figures B & C*

**2.** Press and topstitch the bottom pocket fabric and lining ⅛″ from the edge of the zipper teeth. *Figure D*

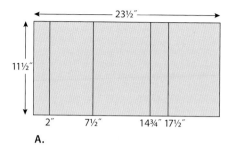

A.

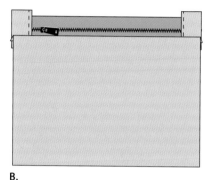

B.

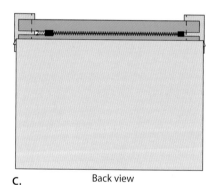

C.          Back view

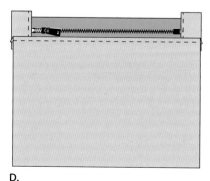

D.

**3.** With the unstitched zipper edge toward you (the zipper is facedown) and the pocket fabrics facing away from you, center the zipper teeth horizontally over the 17½″ mark on your lining main panel. Pin the zipper in place facedown. Stitch the unstitched zipper edge to the lining fabric. *Figure E*

**4.** Press one of the zipper facing pieces in half lengthwise, and then fold each long raw edge in again to meet the middle. This is similar to the method used to make a 4-Fold Open-End Strap (page 10). Press. Pin the facing over the unstitched edge of the zipper so it overlaps onto the lining fabric main panel and covers the previous stitches. Stitch the facing down on both long edges. *Figure F*

**5.** Pinch together the bottom right corner of both pocket pieces to form points about 1″ deep and 1″ wide, with the *right sides* of the bottom pocket fabric touching. Pin in place. *Figure G*

> ### NOTE
> While this is pinned, flip the pouch right side out to test the shape. Does it fit the curves of the bottom edge of the main panel? If not, adjust your pins.

**6.** From the lining side, stitch a vertical line through all 4 layers of bottom pocket fabric at pin marks to make a dart. Repeat on the other corner. Reinforce both seams with an extra line of stitching. *Figure H*

**7.** Snip off the folded points, leaving a ¼″ seam allowance. Finish the edges of the dart seams with a zigzag stitch or serger and turn the corners *right side* out. *Figure I*

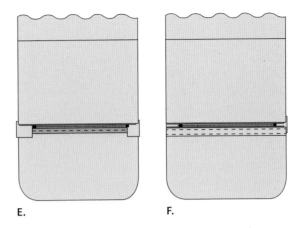

E.    F.

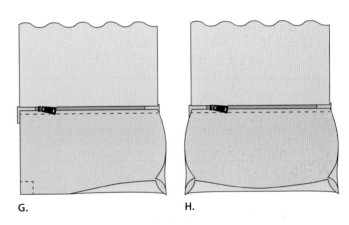

G.    H.

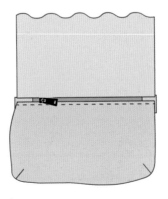

I.

## Make the Mesh Pocket

**1.** Pinch the fold-over elastic (FOE) so it wraps around both sides of one long raw edge of the mesh. Starting at the left side, stitch the FOE to the mesh ⅛″ from the nonfolded edge, stretching the FOE as you sew. Do not stretch the mesh, but instead try to keep it moving at a steady pace. This will add fullness to the pocket.

**2.** Center the mesh pocket (which will be wider than your main panels) so the elastic is on the 7½″ line and bottom edge is on the 14¾″ line. Place the left and right edges of the mesh pocket along the sides of the main panel, or just over the edge, if the elastic stretched wider than the panel. Baste the edges in place. *Figure A*

**3.** Stitch the mesh pocket down the center, separating it into 2 pockets. Baste the bottom of the mesh to the lining, gathering the fabric with your fingers as you go to even out the fullness. Trim off the left and right sides of the mesh pocket to fit the main panel, if needed.

**4.** Prepare one more of the facing pieces as in Step 4 of Make the Bottom Zipper Pocket (page 71). Pin it along the bottom edge of the mesh pocket, covering the raw edges. Stitch down both long edges to secure it to the lining main panel. *Figure B*

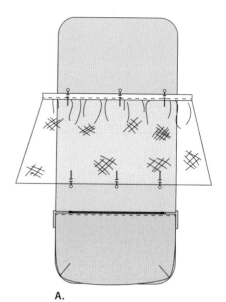

**A.**

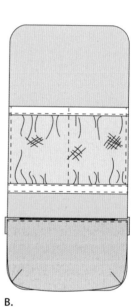

**B.**

## Make the Small Zipper Pocket

**1.** Repeat Steps 1–4 from Make the Bottom Zipper Pocket, (page 70). In Step 3, center the unstitched edge of your zipper horizontally over the 2″ mark on your lining main panel instead of the 17½″ mark. *Figure C*

**2.** Prepare a new facing. Center and pin the facing over the raw edges of the pocket and lining fabrics and stitch the facing down on both long edges to seal the bottom of the pocket. *Figure D*

## Add Elastic and Bias Binding

**1.** Fold the regular elastic in half and pin both ends to the *right side* of the lining, centered above the top zipper pocket. Baste ⅛″ from edge, stitching over the elastic several times to secure it in place. *Figure E*

**2.** With *wrong sides together*, stack the outer main panel and lining main panel. Baste around the perimeter of the organizer ⅛″ from the raw edge.

**3.** Make and apply bias binding for the entire organizer, as instructed in Bias Binding and Piping (page 15).

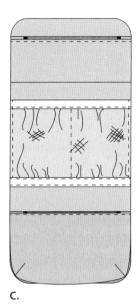

C.

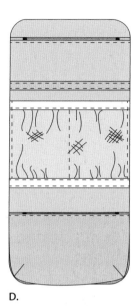

D.

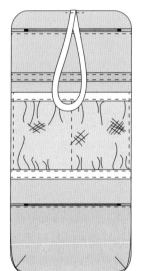

E.

Made by Janelle MacKay

# Two-Bottle Tote

**Finished size:** 10˝ wide × 14¼˝ high × 4˝ deep

*Fabric: Tartan in Aquamarine by Joel Dewberry, FreeSpirit Fabric*

Whether bringing a hostess gift to the neighbors, shopping at the wine store, or going to an outdoor barbecue, I have always felt a bit uncomfortable lugging a bottle of wine or two in a crinkled brown paper bag. Not stylish! This tall, classy, and unnoticeably deceptive tote can handle two very large bottles—one for you and one for the neighbor, too. It's padded inside and has a handy divider that can easily be flipped to the side, so the bag can play double-duty as a shopping tote or large carryall.

**Use it for:**

- Beverage bottles
- Groceries
- Housewarming gifts

## MATERIALS AND SUPPLIES

- **Quilting cotton:** 44˝ wide

  *Outer fabric:* ½ yard

  *Outer accent fabric:* ⅓ yard (or use linen or home decor fabric)

  *Lining fabric:* ½ yard

- **Interfacing:** 1¾ yard of 20˝-wide light- to medium-weight, woven, fusible interfacing (such as Pellon Shape-Flex SF101)

- **Stabilizers:**

  *Heavyweight:* 10˝ × 6˝ of one-sided, fusible heavyweight interfacing or stabilizer (such as Pellon Peltex 71F)

  *Lightweight:* 1 piece of 16˝ × 41˝ lightweight stabilizer (such as ByAnnie's Soft and Stable, Automotive headliner foam, or a fusible needled fleece)

- **Sew-in hook-and-loop tape:** 8˝ length

- **Rectangular rings or D-rings:** 1˝ size, 2 for bag strap

- **Strap buckle with center bar and pin:** ¾˝ size

- **Magnetic purse snap:** ¾˝ size

- **Eyelets with setting tool:** 2, ³⁄₁₆˝ size

- **Water-soluble fabric marker**

- **Walking foot for sewing machine**

# Cutting

*All cutting measurements are listed as width × height, unless otherwise stated.*

## Outer fabric

- Cut 2 squares 15″ × 15″ for external side panels.
- Cut 1 rectangle 10¾″ × 4¾″ for external base.
- Cut 2 rectangles 15″ × 4″ for internal facings.
- Cut 2 rectangles 4¼″ × 3″ for strap tabs.

## Outer accent fabric

- Cut 2 strips 4″ × 12″ for belt straps.
- Cut 1 strip 4½″ × 27″ for shoulder strap.

## Lining fabric

- Cut 1 rectangle 15″ × 11½″ for lining side A.
- Cut 2 rectangles 7⅞″ × 11½″ for lining side B.
- Cut 2 rectangles 5½″ × 10″ for divider.
- Cut 1 rectangle 10½″ × 4¾″ for lining base.

## Interfacing

*Interfacing pieces can be cut ½″–1″ smaller than listed in order to reduce bulk in the seams.*

- Cut 2 squares 15″ × 15″ for external side panels.
- Cut 2 rectangles 10¾″ × 4¾″ for external base (cut full size; do not reduce).
- Cut 2 rectangles 15″ × 4″ for internal facings.
- Cut 1 rectangle 15″ × 11½″ for lining side A.
- Cut 2 rectangles 7⅞″ × 11½″ for lining side B.

## Stabilizers

- Cut 2 squares 15″ × 15″ of lightweight stabilizer for external panels.
- Cut 1 rectangle 5½″ × 10″ of lightweight stabilizer for divider.
- Cut 1 rectangle 10¾″ × 4¾″ of lightweight stabilizer for lining base.
- Cut 1 rectangle 9¾″ × 4″ of heavyweight stabilizer for external base.
- Cut 2 squares 1½″ × 1½″ of heavyweight stabilizer for magnetic snap insertion.

# Instructions

*All seam allowances are ⅜″ unless otherwise noted.*

## Fuse Interfacing and Attach Stabilizer

Follow the manufacturer's directions to fuse interfacing to the *wrong side* of the coordinating pieces.

### Attach the Soft and Stable

**1.** With *right sides up*, place the exterior panels onto the lightweight stabilizer. Pin every few inches, around the perimeter.

**2.** Machine baste around the edges using a ¼″ seam allowance and a long basting stitch.

**3.** Carefully trim next to your basting stitches, cutting away all the stabilizer from the seam allowances.

**4.** Repeat Steps 1–3 for the lining base piece.

> **NOTE**
>
> For the exterior base you will fuse one piece of the woven interfacing to the *wrong side* of the fabric piece first. Then center the fusible heavyweight stabilizer on this, and cover it with the second layer of woven interfacing. Spritz with water and use steam to press through all 4 layers. The 1½″ square of fusible heavyweight interfacing for the magnetic snap will be used later in the instructions.

## Assemble the Exterior Bag

### Make the Shoulder Strap

**1.** Refer to 4-Fold Closed-End Strap (page 11) to make the shoulder strap.

**2.** Repeat the top stitching ⅛″ from the first stitching line to make 2 rows of top stitching around the strap.

**3.** Slide a 1″ metal ring onto one end and fold the end over 1½″. Sew a box with an X through it to secure the strap end to the strap.

**4.** Repeat Step 3 for the other end of the strap.

## Make the Belt

**1.** Refer to 4-Fold Closed-End Strap (page 11), closing only one end and leaving the other open, on one of the 12″ belt straps. Edgestitch ⅛″ from the edge on all folded edges.

**2.** With the strap in front of you so that the long, folded edge is on top and the seam is on the bottom, mark a placement dot on the strap 1½″ from the closed end, centered.

**3.** Insert one eyelet on the placement dot, following the manufacturer's directions.

**4.** Insert the eyelet end of the strap onto the buckle, as shown, and fold the end to the back. Pull taut and stitch across the end of the strap to secure.

**5.** Working on the other 12″ piece, fold back ¼″ on one of the short sides to the *wrong side* and press.

**6.** Fold the entire strip in half lengthwise and press.

**7.** To make a pointed end, open again and, working on the end that has the ¼″ pressed over, fold the outer corners toward the center fold line, creating 45° angles.

**8.** Trim away inside corners to reduce bulk, leaving about a ½″ seam allowance.

**9.** Fold the outside edges toward the center fold mark and press.

**10.** Refold the strip in half, meeting the folded edges together, and press.

**11.** Topstitch around the perimeter ⅛″ from the outer edge.

**12.** Working on the pointed strap, mark a placement dot on the strap 3¾″ from the point, centered.

**13.** Insert an eyelet on the placement dot.

**14.** Insert the pointed strap into the buckle of the other strap.

## Assemble the Exterior Panels

**1.** Place the belt on the front of one of your exterior panels, with the top edge of the belt 3½″ down from the top edge of the panel. Make sure the belt buckle is perfectly centered. Pin in place.

**2.** Baste in place in the left and right side seam allowances.

**3.** Anchor the belt in place by topstitching vertical lines on each strap about 1½″ on either side of the belt buckle. *Figure A*

**4.** Trim off the belt ends so they are even with the side edges.

**5.** Place the exterior panels together, *right sides together*, and sew the side seams, leaving the top and bottom open. Using a pressing cloth and a warm iron, press the side seams open.

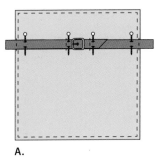

**A.**

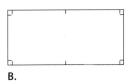

**B.**

## Attach the Base

**1.** Mark start/stop lines ⅜″ in from all 4 corners on the *wrong side* of the exterior base. Measure and mark the center of each side on the exterior base, as well as the top and bottom edges on the exterior side panels. *Figure B*

**2.** With *right sides together*, place one long side of the base along the bottom edge of one exterior panel, match the center marks, and pin together.

**3.** Stitch from the start/stop markings at one corner to the start/stop markings at the end, making sure to not sew past these marks.

**4.** Repeat for the other side. *Figure C*

**5.** Center each side seam of the exterior panel on a short end of the base and pin in place. Make a small clip in the seam allowance of the side panel where the corner will be. Sew across the end of the base from edge to edge. Repeat for the other side. *Figure D*

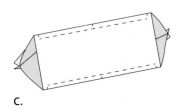

**C.**

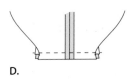

**D.**

**1.** Refer to 4-Fold Open-End Strap (page 10) to create 2 small tabs from the 2 strap tab rectangles.

> **NOTE**
>
> The 4¼″ measurement is the width and the 3″ measurement is the length.

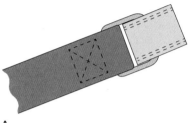

**A.**

**2.** Repeat the top stitching ⅛″ from the first stitching line to make 2 rows of top stitching to match the shoulder strap.

**3.** Slide 1 strap tab onto 1 metal ring that is attached to the shoulder strap and baste the ends closed using a ⅛″ seam allowance. Repeat with the other strap tab. *Figure A*

**4.** Center the strap tabs over the *right side* of the exterior bag side seams, matching raw edges, and pin to secure. Baste the strap tabs in place using a ¼″ seam allowance. *Figure B*

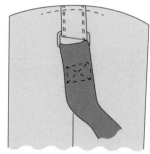

**B.**

## Assemble the Lining

**1.** Using a ¼″ seam allowance, baste the lightweight stabilizer onto the wrong side of 1 fabric divider piece.

**2.** Place the 2 divider pieces together, *right sides together*, pin, and stitch around both short ends and one long side, leaving one long side open for turning.

**3.** Clip the corners, trim the seam allowances to ⅛″, and turn the divider *right side out*. Press.

**4.** Topstitch around the sewn sides ⅛″ from the edge.

**5.** Sew a vertical line of stitching, lengthwise on the divider, 1″ from the side without raw edges. Then stitch another line ⅛″ on the other side of that (1⅛″ from the edge) to make 2 lines side by side. *Figure C*

**6.** Center the divider between the 2 lining side B pieces. *Right sides* should be facing together and the raw edges on the sides of all 3 pieces should be aligned. Stitch through all layers to create 1 side panel with the divider flap protruding from the center. Press the seam open. *Figure D*

### Attach the Hook-and-Loop Tape

**1.** Fold the lining side A piece in half crosswise and finger press to make a fold line. Unfold *right side up* and place the loop side of the hook-and-loop tape on the left side of the fold line, centered from top to bottom, and stitch in place. *Figure E*

**2.** With the lining side B in front of you, fold the center divider to the right and place the hook side of the tape in the 1″ section on the right edge of the divider. Center it from top to bottom, and stitch in place. *Figure F*

### Attach the Magnetic Snap

Attach 1 magnetic snap (page 13) side to the center of each of the internal facing pieces.

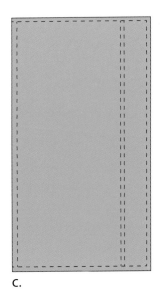

C.

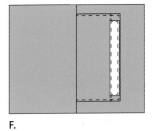

D.

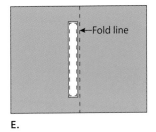

E.        F.

←Fold line

**1.** Sew 1 facing piece to the top of each lining panel. Press the seams toward the facing and topstitch on the facing side of the seam.

> ### NOTE
>
> The top of the side panel with the divider attached will be top edge when viewing it in the illustration in Attach the Hook-and-Loop Tape (page 81). The divider is flipped to the right, and the tape is on the front right of the divider.
>
>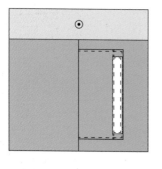

**2.** Place the lining panels together, *right sides together*, and stitch the side seams, leaving an opening of 7″ on one side for turning. Press the side seams open.

**3.** Refer to Attach the Base (page 79) to attach the lining base.

**4.** To reinforce stitches and reduce bulk, after the base is attached, sew an extra round of stitching around the perimeter, stitching ⅛″ away from the first line. Trim corners and seam allowances to ⅛″.

## Attach Exterior to Lining

**1.** With the lining *wrong side out* and the bag exterior *right side out*, slide the bag exterior into the lining. Match the side seams and centers and pin around the bag opening.

**2.** Using a ⅜″ seam allowance, sew around the bag opening. Turn the bag *right side out* using the turning hole in the lining. Sew the lining hole closed by machine with a 1⁄16″ seam allowance or use an invisible slip stitch by hand. Push the lining down inside the bag exterior.

**3.** Press the seam around the bag opening and topstitch around the bag opening to finish.

Made by Sara Lawson

# Tablet Shoulder Bag

**Finished size:** 7¼″ wide × 10″ long × 2½″ deep

*Fabric: Fox Field by Tula Pink, FreeSpirit Fabric*

A friend of mine requested a bag specifically for her iPad, so I designed this padded shoulder bag that's the perfect size for carrying a tablet device. Technology is ever changing, but this bag is designed to grow with you. A smaller inside pocket holds smaller-sized devices, while the bag body can hold a larger tablet or anything else you'd like to tote around, such as headphones, a charger, or your cell phone. A pocket flap with a magnetic snap keeps the contents safe and locked away.

**Use it for:**

- Electronics
- Lightweight carryall

## PATTERN PIECES

*Refer to Pattern Pieces (page 6).*

- Tablet Shoulder Bag Front Pocket (pattern pullout page P2)
- Tablet Shoulder Bag Flap (pattern pullout page P2)

## MATERIALS AND SUPPLIES

- **Quilting cotton:** 44˝ wide

  *For outer fabric:* ½ yard

  *For lining fabric:* ¾ yard

  *For straps and front accent:* ¼ yard

- **Interfacing:** 1⅜ yards of light- to medium-weight, woven, fusible interfacing (such as Pellon Shape-Flex SF101)

- **Stabilizer:** ½ yard light-weight stabilizer (such as ByAnnie's Soft and Stable or substitute Pellon Thermolam fusible interfacing)

- **Metal rectangle rings:** 2, 1˝ diameter

- **Metal adjustable slider:** 1˝ size, for strap

- **Magnetic snap:** ½˝ size

# Cutting

*All measurements are width × height.*

## Outer fabric:

- Cut 1 front pocket on the fold.
- Cut 1 bag flap on the fold.
- Cut 2 rectangles 11˝ × 12½˝ for the bag front and bag back.

## Lining fabric:

- Cut 1 lining front pocket on the fold.
- Cut 1 lining flap on the fold.
- Cut 2 rectangles 11˝ × 12½˝ for the lining front and lining back.
- Cut 2 rectangles 11˝ × 10˝ for the lining pocket.

## Straps and front accent fabric:

- Cut 1 rectangle 42˝ × 4˝ for the strap.
- Cut 1 rectangle 3˝ × 4˝ for the strap extender.
- Cut 2 rectangles 7½˝ × 1½˝ for the flap tab.

## Interfacing:

- Cut 1 front pocket on the fold.
- Cut 1 exterior flap on the fold.
- Cut 1 rectangle 42˝ × 3˝ for the strap.
- Cut 1 rectangle 3˝ × 4˝ for the strap extender.
- Cut 2 rectangles 7½˝ × 1½˝ for the flap tab.
- Cut 2 rectangles 11˝ × 12½˝ for the lining front and lining back.

## Stabilizer:

- Cut 1 front pocket on the fold.
- Cut 1 flap on the fold.
- Cut 2 rectangles 11˝ × 12½˝ for the bag front and bag back.
- Cut 1 rectangle 11˝ × 10˝ for the lining pocket.

Two-Bottle Tote
(page 74)

Airport Sling
(page 109)

Snap-and-Go
Sewing or Art Case
(page 121)

Tablet Shoulder Bag
(page 83)

# Instructions

*All seam allowances are ½" unless otherwise noted.*

## Fuse the Interfacing and Stabilizer

**1.** Place the bag front with the *wrong side* of the fabric against the stabilizer. Pin in place. Baste around the outer edge of the fabric using a ⅛" seam allowance. Repeat for the bag back, lining flap, bag front pocket, and 1 lining pocket.

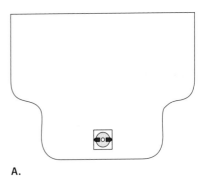

**A.**

## Tip

**Gently pull your fabric taut as you baste it to the stabilizer for a tight, crisp finish. If you would like, machine quilt the stabilizer pieces at this time.**

**2.** Place the fusible (tacky) side of the interfacing against the *wrong side* of the strap. Fuse according to the manufacturer's instructions. Repeat for the lining front and back, exterior flap, lining front pocket, strap extender, and flap tabs.

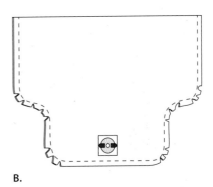

**B.**

## Assemble the Flap and Front Pocket

**1.** Find the center of the bottom curved edge of the lining flap. On the wrong side, measure 1" up from the curve, and mark the prong placement for the smaller half of the magnetic snap. Attach the magnetic snap (page 13). *Figure A*

**2.** Place the bag flap and the lining flap *right sides* together. Sew along the flap, leaving the top straight edge unsewn, using a ¼" seam allowance. Notch the seam allowance around the curves. *Figure B*

**C.**

**3.** Turn the completed flap *right side out* and press. Edgestitch the finished edge ⅛" from edge. *Figure C*

**4.** On the right side of the fabric, measure and mark the prong placement for the larger half of the magnetic snap, centered and down 2" from the top straight edge of the bag front pocket. Attach the magnetic snap (page 13). *Figure D*

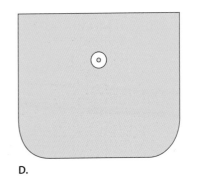

**D.**

## Attach the Flap and Flap Tabs

**1.** Place the right side of the bag flap against the right side of the bag back with raw edges aligned and the flap centered. Pin and then baste the flap in place using a ¼″ seam allowance.

**2.** Sew the 2 flap tab pieces *right sides* together along both long edges using a ¼″ seam allowance. Turn them right side out and press. Edgestitch the finished edges ⅛″ from edge. *Figure A*

A.

**3.** Place the flap tab ½″ down from the top edge of the bag front pocket, aligned with the left and right raw edge of the front pocket. Baste the flap tab in place on both ends using a ⅛″ seam allowance. *Figure B*

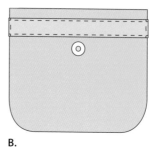

B.

**4.** Place the bag front pocket and lining front pocket *right sides* together. Sew along the outer edge of the front pocket using a ¼″ seam allowance, leaving a 5″ opening along the top straight edge. Clip the corners and notch the curved edges. *Figure C*

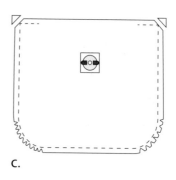

C.

**5.** Turn the front pocket *right side out* and press, also pressing in the opening toward the *wrong side* by ¼″. Edgestitch along the top edge ⅛″ from the edge. *Figure D*

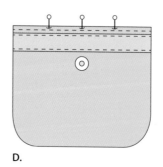

D.

**6.** Draw a horizontal line on the right side of the bag front 3½″ from the top edge. Place the front pocket, *right side up*, at this line and centered. Sew the sides and bottom of the front pocket using a ⅛″ seam allowance. (You will be sewing on top of the flap tabs too). *Figure E*

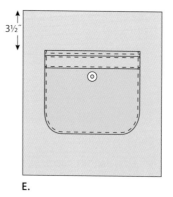

3½″

E.

## Assemble the Lining

**1.** Place the lining pocket pieces *right sides* together. Sew along only the top and bottom 11″ edges using a ¼″ seam allowance.

**2.** Turn the lining pocket *right side out* and press. Topstitch the top and bottom edges using a ⅛″ seam allowance.

**3.** Draw a line on the right side of the lining back 1½″ from the top edge. Place the top edge of the lining pocket at this line. Edgestitch the side and bottom edges of the lining pocket a ⅛″ from the edge. *Figure A*

## Assemble the Exterior and Lining

**1.** Measure to mark a 1¼″ square at each bottom corner of the bag front. Cut out each square. Repeat this step for the bag back. *Figure B*

**2.** Place both the bag front and the bag back *right sides together*. Pin and sew along the sides and bottom, leaving the top edge and the cut-out squares unsewn. *Figure C*

**3.** Pinch the bottom left corner so that the raw edges are aligned and the side seams match up. Sew the 2 raw edges. Repeat for the right corner. *Figures D & E*

**4.** Repeat Steps 1–3 for the lining, except leave a 6″ opening at the bottom.

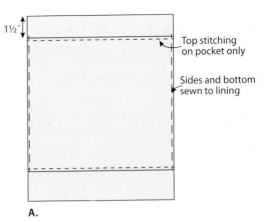

1½″

Top stitching on pocket only

Sides and bottom sewn to lining

A.

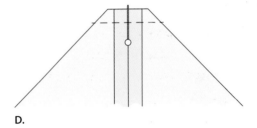

B.

C.

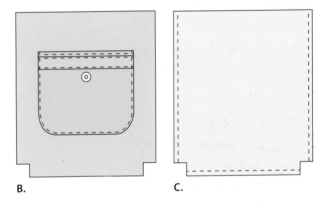

D.

Open for turning

E.

## Make the Strap

**1.** Refer to the 4-Fold Open-End Strap method (page 10) to make a strap. Topstitch along both long edges, ⅛" from each edge.

**2.** Repeat Step 1 for the strap extender piece.

**3.** Turn the bag *right side out*. Slide the metal rectangle onto the strap extender and fold the strap extender in half. Place the strap extender centered on the outside of the left side seam of the bag. The raw edges of the strap extender should be aligned with the top raw edge of the bag. Baste in place using a ¼" seam allowance.

**4.** Refer to Adjustable Strap (page 12), except in Step 1, fold the end of the strap over ½" after threading it over the bar of the adjustable slider. Stitch the raw edge within the box. Thread the other end of the strap through the extender piece and back through the adjustable slider. Then baste the end centered over the right side seam of the bag.

## Finish the Bag

**1.** With the lining inside out, slide the lining over the bag so the pieces are *right sides together* and the straps are between them. The lining pocket should be on the same side as the flap. Align the top edges, making sure to also line up the side seams. Pin in place. Stitch all along the top edge of the bag.

**2.** Turn the bag *right side out* through the opening in the lining. Press. Topstitch the top edge of the bag using a ⅛" seam allowance.

**3.** Slipstitch or topstitch the opening in the lining closed.

Made by Lindsay Conner

# Sporty Strap Pack

**Finished size:** 13˝ × 18⅝˝

*Fabric: Robert Kaufman Essex Linen; Wildwood by Elizabth Olwen, Cloud9 Fabrics*

While lugging around an infant car seat, I unknowingly dropped my belongings in parking lots all over town. My cell phone, a mega-pack of paper towels, and the very shirt I left the house to buy—all were returned, thanks to the kindness of strangers. This one-shoulder backpack keeps belongings nearby so your hands are free to multitask (or even to walk the dog). Wear it across the body with the zipper facing in or out for easy access. Two pockets (one outside, one inside) will keep your wallet, keys, and phone organized. This sleek, unisex design can be customized with interchangeable pocket styles and your choice of fabric.

**Use it for:**

- **Hands-free carryall**
- **Dog leash, water, and treats**
- **Toddler snacks and toys**
- **Change of clothes**

## PATTERN PIECES

*Refer to Pattern Pieces (page 6).*

- Sporty Strap Pack Body (pattern pullout page P1)
- Corner (pattern pullout page P2) (*Refer to Curved Corners, page 7.*)

## MATERIALS AND SUPPLIES

- **Quilting cotton:**

  *For outer fabric:* 1 yard

  *For lining fabric:* ⅝ yard

- **Interfacing:** 2 yards of 20˝-wide light- to medium-weight, woven, fusible interfacing (such as Pellon Shape-Flex SF101 or Fusible Featherweight 911FF)

- **Stabilizer:** 1 yard of 45˝-wide extra lofty, one-sided fusible, needled fleece (such as Pellon TP971F Fusible Thermolam Plus)

- **Nylon strapping:** 1˝ wide, 19˝ length—cut into 7˝ for top strap and 12˝ for lower strap

- **Adjustable slider:** 1˝ plastic for bag strap or side release buckle

- **Elastic:** ½˝ wide, 10˝ length

- **Metal purse snap:** ½˝ or larger

- **Zipper:** 16˝ length, all-purpose

# Cutting

## Outer fabrics:

- Cut 2 body pieces. (Cut once through folded fabric to get front and back in reverse.)
- Cut 2 strips 3½″ × 19½″ for top strap.
- Cut 2 strips 3½″ × 6½″ for lower strap.
- Cut 2 pieces 7½″ (wide) × 4″ (tall) for pocket flap.
- Cut 2 pieces 7″ (wide) × 9″ (tall) for flat pocket.
- Cut 1 piece 3″ × 19″ for zipper flap.
- Cut 2 pieces 3″ × 1½″ for zipper tabs.
- Cut 1 piece 3″ × 6¼″ for strap facing.

## Lining fabrics:

- Cut 2 body pieces. (Cut once through folded fabric to get front and back in reverse.)
- Cut 2 pieces 8″ × 10″ for gathered pocket.

> **NOTE**
> See Hint (page 97) for ideas on switching pocket styles.

## Interfacing:

- Cut 2 body pieces. (Cut once through folded fabric to get front and back in reverse.)
- Cut 2 strips 3½″ × 19½″ for top strap.
- Cut 2 strips 3½″ × 6½″ for lower strap.
- Cut 2 pieces 8″ × 10″ for gathered pocket.
- Cut 2 pieces 7″ × 9″ for flat pocket.
- Cut 2 pieces 7½″ × 4″ for pocket flap.
- Cut 1 piece 3″ × 19″ for zipper flap.
- Cut 1 piece 3″ × 6¼″ for strap facing.

## Stabilizer:

- Cut 2 body pieces. (Cut once through folded fabric to get front and back in reverse.)
- Cut 1 strip 3″ × 19″ for top strap.
- Cut 1 strip 3″ × 6″ for lower strap.
- Cut 1 piece 8″ × 10″ for gathered pocket.
- Cut 1 piece 7″ × 9″ for flat pocket.
- Cut 1 piece 7½″ × 4″ pocket flap.

# Instructions

*All seam allowances are ⅜″ unless otherwise noted.*

## Fuse Fabrics

**1.** Fuse interfacing to the *wrong side* of 2 body lining pieces, top strap, lower strap, flat pocket, pocket flap, zipper flap, strap facing, and gathered pocket.

**2.** Fuse stabilizer to the *wrong side* of matching pieces cut from the main fabric including 2 body pieces, 1 flat pocket, 1 pocket flap, and 1 gathered pocket (do not fuse on the top strap or lower strap yet).

## Make the Straps

**1.** Fold both top strap pieces in half lengthwise with *wrong sides together* and press. With the strap folded, use a rotary cutter to round the corner of one short raw edge. The strap should have a gentle U shape when opened. (If you would rather not do this freehand, use the 2″ marking on the corner template as a guide.) Repeat with one end of the lower strap so the curves match.

> **NOTE**
>
> If using a directional print, make sure to round the bottom corners of the top strap and the top corners of the bottom strap.

**2.** Round the corners of one short edge of the top and lower stabilizer pieces in the same manner. Center and fuse the stabilizer to the *wrong side* of 1 top strap and 1 lower strap, leaving a ¼″ seam allowance open on all sides except the top edge. *Figure A*

**3.** Pin the nylon strapping to the *right side* of the remaining top strap piece (nonstabilized) so that the strapping extends just ½″ over the curved end. Baste the strapping in place ⅛″ from the end of the strap. *Figure B*

**4.** Pin both top strap pieces together, *right sides facing*, and stitch around the long edge, the curve, and the other long edge, leaving the flat short end open for turning. Turn the top strap *right side out*, using the nylon strap to pull. Press. *Figure C*

**A.**

3½″

**B.**

**C.**

**5.** Topstitch the top strap ⅛″ and then ¼″ from the perimeter, leaving the raw edge open.

**6.** Threading front to back, thread the raw edge of the strapping through the top rung of the side release buckle. If using the strap adjuster, fold over 1½″ and pin in place. Stitch a box with an X in it to secure to the back of the strapping. *Figure D*

**7.** Repeat Steps 3–5 to sew the lower strap.

**8.** Thread the lower strap through the side release buckle or the strap adjuster.

**9.** Baste both straps to the *right side* of the outer body piece with *double notches on the left and single notch on right*, as pictured in the drawing below, sewing ⅛″ from edge. *Figure E*

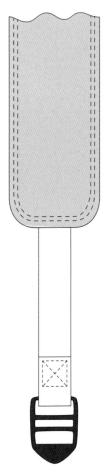

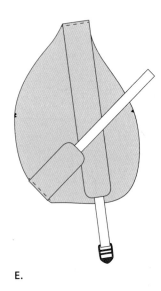

E.

D.

# Make the Pockets

## Make the Elastic Pocket

**1.** Stack both elastic pocket pieces and fold in half crosswise. Use a rotary cutter to round the 2 bottom corners to make a gentle curve. (If you would rather not do this freehand, use the 5¼″ marking on the corner template, as a guide.)

**2.** With the *right sides facing*, sew the pocket pieces together around the perimeter with a ¼″ seam allowance. Leave a 3″ opening at the bottom for turning. Trim the corners and clip the curves. Turn the pocket *right side out* and press.

**3.** Stitch a line ¾″ from the straight pocket top to make an elastic casing. Use a seam ripper to remove the stitches within the side seams on both sides. *Figure A*

**4.** Attach a safety pin to one end of the elastic and feed it through the casing. Baste the loose end of elastic to the pocket ⅛″ from the side seam to hold it in place. Pull the elastic and gather the fabric so that the casing is 6½″ wide on top. Baste the elastic ⅛″ from the edge and remove the safety pin. Trim the excess elastic. *Figure B*

**5.** Center the pocket on the lining body with the *single notch on the left and double notches on the right*, and topstitch the sides and bottom in place ⅛″ and ¼″ from the edge, leaving the top elastic part open. *Figure C*

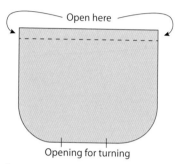

Open here

Opening for turning

**A.**

**B.**

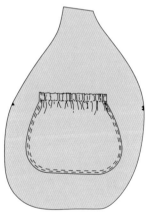

**C.**

## Make the Flat Pocket

**1.** Set aside the flat pocket while you make the pocket flap. Stack both 7½″ × 4″ rectangles and fold in half. Use a rotary cutter to round corners on a 7½″ side. (If you would rather not do this freehand, use the 6″ marking on the Corner pattern, pullout page P2, as a guide.) *Figure D*

**2.** Attach 1 magnetic snap (page 13) to the stabilized pocket and pocket flap. Center one side of the snap 2½″ down from the top of the pocket and the other side of the snap 1″ up from the bottom curve of the pocket flap.

**3.** With *right sides facing*, sew the pocket pieces together around the perimeter with a ¼″ seam allowance. Leave a 3″ opening at the top flat edge for turning. Trim the corners and curves. Turn the pocket *right side out* and press. Repeat with the pocket flap pieces. *Figure E*

**4.** Topstitch the pocket ⅛″ and ¼″ across the top straight edge. Topstitch the pocket flap ¼″ from the sides and curved bottom edge. *Figure F*

**5.** Position the pocket (metal snap facing up) on the *right side* of the outer body with the straps attached. Measure up 2″ from the bottom and place the pocket between the horizontal 2″ and 8½″ marks along that line. Topstitch the sides and bottom of the pocket ¼″ from the edge. *Figure G*

**6.** Position the straight edge of the pocket flap (metal snap facing down) just above the top of the pocket. Pin it in place and let the magnets connect. Topstitch the pocket flap in place ¼″ from the straight edge. *Figure H*

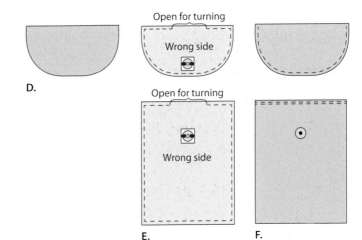

D.

Open for turning
Wrong side

E.

Open for turning
Wrong side

F.

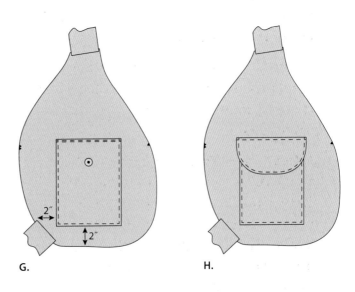

G.

H.

**Hint** Switch out the gathered and flat pockets and use them with or without the same flap to customize your backpack.

*Option:* Switch the placement of the gathered and flat pockets.

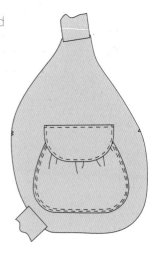

## Attach the Zipper

**1.** Stack the remaining lining and outer body pieces *right sides together*. With the lining *on the top*, measure 1½″ across the top neck of the lining and mark. Line up your ruler straight down from your previous mark so that it runs approximately to the center of the bag bottom. Cut straight through both panels to separate the outer and lining into 2 pieces each, to allow for the zipper insertion. *Figure A*

**Hint** ▸ To make the seams of this bag less bulky around the zipper, it's helpful to trim the stabilizer back just a bit. To do this, peel back the stabilizer along the straight edge you just cut and carefully snip away ¼″ of stabilizer. Repeat on the straight edge of the other panel.

**2.** Fold the zipper flap in half lengthwise, with *wrong sides together*, and press.

**3.** Sew the zipper tabs to each end of the zipper as described in the Airport Sling project, Attach the Zipper Pocket, Step 1 (page 114), except use the 3″ × 1½″ tabs.

**4.** With the left outer body piece *right side up and with the single notch on the left side*, place the zipper flap on top so that all raw edges are aligned. Place the zipper *facedown* on the zipper flap so that the right edges are aligned.

**5.** Place the corresponding lining piece (with one notch) *wrong side up* over this, aligning the straight edge with the zipper edge and other body piece below.

**6.** Pin together through all layers along the zipper edge (or use double-sided wash-away tape) and stitch ¼″ from the right edge. *Figure B*

**7.** Press the body pieces back, away from the zipper, so the back sides are facing together. Press these back, with the zipper flap pressed over the zipper. Topstitch ⅛″ and then ¼″ to the left of the zipper flap, going through the exterior fabric, zipper, and lining. *Figure C*

**8.** With the right outer body piece *right side up and with the double notch on the right side*, place the unit from Step 7 *wrong side up* over this, aligning the straight edge with the zipper edge. Your zipper should be facedown. *Figure D*

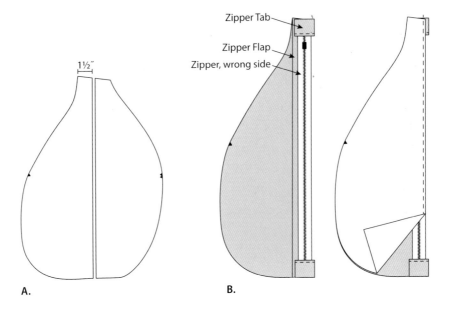

A.

Zipper Tab

Zipper Flap

Zipper, wrong side

B.

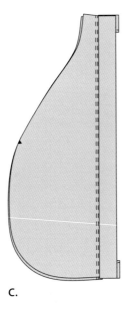

C.

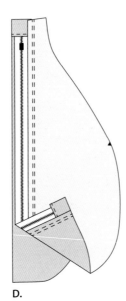

D.

**9.** Place the remaining lining piece (with double notch) *wrong side up* over this, aligning the straight edge with the zipper edge and other body piece below. Pin or tape together through all layers along the zipper edge and stitch ¼˝ from the right edge. *Figure E*

**10.** Press these body pieces back, away from the zipper, and topstitch to the right of the zipper, going through the exterior fabric, zipper, and lining, just as you did in Step 7. *Figure F*

## Finishing the Backpack

### Join the Panels

**1.** Leave the zipper halfway unzipped. Pin the straps to the center of the outer bag panel so that they are out of the way. Place the outer panels *right sides together*, folding the lining to the middle, and pin along all edges.

**2.** Stitch around the perimeter, leaving a hole at the top neck but stitching across the bottom of the zipper tab to close the seam. You should lift your presser foot and readjust the needle when stitching near the bag bottom and zipper seam, so as not to stitch over the lining. *Figure G*

**3.** Pin together the lining panels and stitch them together just as you did with the exterior, but leave a 7˝ gap in the bottom of the lining for turning.

**4.** Turn the bag *right side out* through the hole in the bottom of the lining. Press the bag exterior and the lining along the seams. Hand stitch the hole in the lining closed.

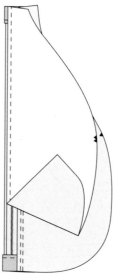

E.

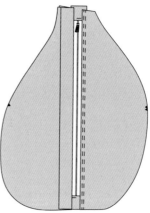

F.

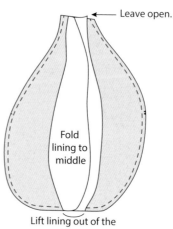

Leave open.

Fold lining to middle

Lift lining out of the way and sew accross.

G.

## Add the Strap Facing

**1.** Press in 2 long edges of the strap facing ¼″ to the *wrong side.* Then sew the facing *right sides together* along one short end to make a loop. *Figure H*

**2.** Flip the facing right side out and slide it over the top strap. Rotate the facing so that the seam lines up with one side seam of the strap.

**3.** Slide the facing so that it overlaps the fabric zipper tab and not the zipper itself. Carefully topstitch the top and bottom of the strap facing, sewing slowly through any bulky seams. *Figure I*

Press over ¼″.

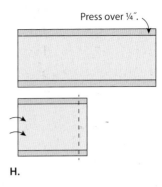

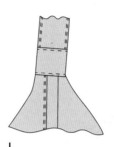

H.

I.

## Tip ←

**Depending on your fabric, the facing may fit too loosely. Adjust the strap facing as needed. You may also sew the facing seam at a slight angle to make it fit the curves of the strap.**

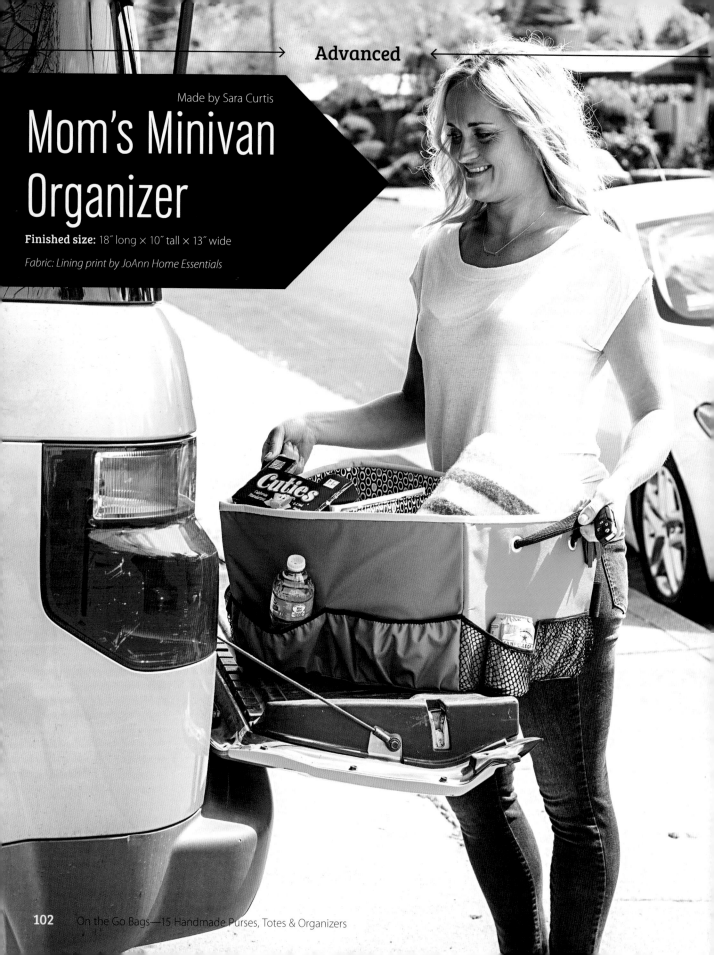

Made by Sara Curtis

# Mom's Minivan Organizer

**Finished size:** 18″ long × 10″ tall × 13″ wide

*Fabric: Lining print by JoAnn Home Essentials*

Our family vehicle is often a dumping ground for loose books, extra diapers and wipes, and assorted gadgets. This box-shaped trunk organizer is great for storing a small camera, wet wipes, pens, loose change, ChapStick, a small first-aid kit, reusable grocery bags, sunglasses, granola bars, sunscreen, and more! For a family vacation, you can load it up with snacks, lunch bags, and paper towels–the elastic loops on the sides are great for holding water bottles.

**Use it for:**

- Road-trip gear
- Snacks and drinks
- Electronics and cords
- Sports equipment

## MATERIALS AND SUPPLIES

- **Indoor/outdoor canvas:** 56″ wide

  *For outer fabric:* 1 yard

  *For lining and divider fabric:* 1 yard

  *For binding:* ¼ yard

- **Mesh pocket fabric:** ¼ yard

- **Interfacing:** 2 yards of one-sided fusible heavyweight interfacing or stabilizer (such as Pellon Peltex 71F)

- **Stabilizer:** 1 yard of one-sided fusible fleece (such as Pellon 987F)

- **Elastic:** 2″ wide, ⅔ yard

- **Fold-over elastic:** 1″ wide or ½″ folded, 2 yards

- **Grommets and setting tools:** 4, ⁷⁄₁₆″ size

- **Sew-on hook-and-loop tape:** 1″ wide, 18″ length

- **Webbing:** 1″-wide cotton webbing, ½ yard

- **Utility knife**

# Cutting

## Outer fabrics

- Cut 2 rectangles 11″ × 19″ for the long sides.

- Cut 2 rectangles 11″ × 14″ for the short sides.

- Cut 1 rectangle 14″ × 19″ for the bottom.

- Cut 2 rectangles 5″ × 24″ for the outer pocket.

## Lining fabrics

- Cut 2 rectangles 11″ × 19″ for the long sides.

- Cut 2 rectangles 11″ × 14″ for the short sides.

- Cut 1 rectangle 14″ × 19″ for the bottom.

- Cut 2 rectangles 11″ × 16″ for the divider.

## Mesh fabric

- Cut 2 rectangles 5″ × 18″ for mesh pockets.

## Binding fabric

- Cut 2 strips 3″ × width of fabric and join end to end following Double-Layer Bias Binding, Steps 2 and 3 (page 15), to make 76″ of binding. (Strips do not have to be cut on the bias.)

## Interfacing and stabilizer

- Cut 2 rectangles of each 10″ × 18″ for the long sides of the lining.

- Cut 2 rectangles of each 10″ × 13″ for the short sides of the lining.

- Cut 1 rectangle of each 13″ × 18″ for the bottom of the lining.

- Cut 1 rectangle of each 10″ × 15″ for the divider.

## Webbing

- Cut 2 strips 9″ long.

# Instructions

*All seam allowances are ½″ unless otherwise noted.*

## Fuse the Interfacing and Stabilizer

*Interfacing and stabilizer pieces are cut 1″ smaller than the corresponding lining pieces and should be centered on your fabric.*

**1.** Place the adhesive side of the interfacing on the *wrong side* of each lining piece and fuse according to the manufacturer's directions. Repeat with the divider piece.

**2.** Place the adhesive side of the stabilizer on the plain side of the interfacing for each lining panel and the divider; then fuse.

## Make the Pockets

**1.** Place the outer pocket pieces *wrong sides together* and sandwich a long edge of the pocket between the fold-over elastic. Use a zigzag stitch to attach the elastic to the pocket, making sure that you stretch the elastic (but not the fabric) very tightly as you sew.

**2.** Gather the other long side by sewing a long basting stitch down the edge with a ⅛″ seam allowance, keeping the thread tails long. Gather the fabric by holding the bobbin thread and sliding the fabric together along its length so that it puckers along the thread.

### NOTE

You'll need only about 12″ of fold-over elastic for each pocket, but it's best to leave the whole length together and cut off the excess after applying. The first time you use fold-over elastic, you might need to practice, so this pattern allots an extra yard. One yard should be enough for this project after you have experience using fold-over elastic.

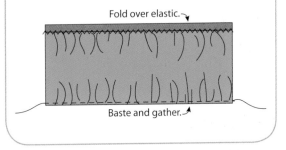

Fold over elastic.

Baste and gather.

**3.** Align the gathered edge of the pocket with a 19″ edge of an outer long side piece. Adjust the gathers to fit.

**4.** Using a ⅛″ seam allowance, baste both layers of the bottom and sides of the pocket to the outer side, pulling the elastic to fit so that the edges match. Sew a vertical line to divide the pocket in half, backstitching to secure the top of the pocket. *Figure A*

**5.** For each mesh pocket, sandwich the ungathered long edges between fold-over elastic as you did in Step 1.

**6.** For each piece, machine baste the other long edge and gather according the method used previously in Step 2. *Figure B*

**7.** Align the long gathered edge of the mesh pocket to one 14″ edge of an outer short side piece. Adjust the gathers to fit. Tie the thread ends to keep the gathers from coming out.

**8.** Baste the bottom and sides of the mesh pocket to the outer short side, pulling the elastic to fit so that the edges match. Sew a vertical line to divide the pocket in half, backstitching to secure the top of the pocket. *Figure C*

**9.** Repeat Steps 7 and 8 to construct and add the mesh pocket to the other short side.

**10.** Fold the remaining long outer side piece in half to find the horizontal center. The long sides will be across the top and bottom, with the short sides on the ends. Mark a dot along that fold at the following points: 5″, 9½″, and 14″.

**11.** Center the 2″ elastic over the horizontal center on the *right side* of the outer piece. Baste the ends of the elastic to the short edges of the outer piece. The elastic will gap in the middle.

**12.** Stitch the elastic vertically at each marking, measuring 6″ of elastic between each 4½″ section to form loops. *Figure D*

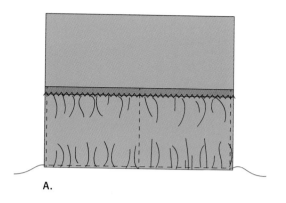

A.

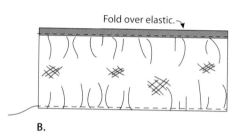

B.

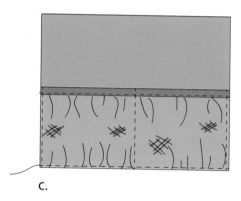

C.

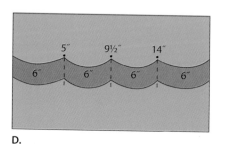

D.

## Make the Organizer

**1.** Stitch the outer rectangles together alternating the short and long sides. For each piece, align with the adjacent rectangle *right sides together*. Stitch and press. Continue until all 4 pieces are stitched together and form a loop.

**2.** With *right sides together*, align each corner of the bottom piece with the 4 seams on the loop you just finished, making sure that the gathered edges of the pockets will be included in the seams. Stitch the bottom piece to the side pieces, pivoting at the corners. Trim the corners and press. *Figure A*

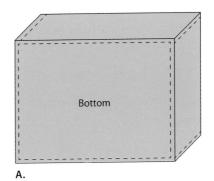

**A.**

## Make the Lining

**1.** On the right side of each of the lining long side pieces, measure 9½″ from the left short side and place a 9″ piece of the soft side of the hook-and-loop tape in place vertically. Topstitch the tape in place on each lining piece. *Figure B*

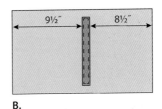

**B.**

**2.** Using the illustration for placement, stitch the lining sides together. For each piece, align with the adjacent rectangle *right sides together*. Stitch and press. *Figure C*

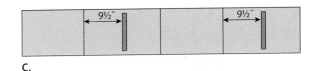

**C.**

**3.** Continue until all 4 pieces are stitched together and form a loop.

**4.** Align each corner of the bottom lining piece with the 4 seams on the loop of rectangles you just finished. Stitch the bottom piece to the side pieces, pivoting at the corners. Trim seams and corners. Press.

## Make the Divider

**1.** Place the 2 divider pieces right sides together. Stitch around all 4 sides, pivoting at the corners and leaving a 5″ opening on one side. Trim the seams and corners.

**2.** Turn the divider rectangle right side out and push the corners out using a knitting needle or point turner.

**3.** Fold and press the raw edges of the opening under ½″. Topstitch ⅛ from the edge around all 4 sides of the divider.

**4.** On each 10″ side of the divider, measure inward 1¼″ and topstitch another line to form flaps for the hook-and-loop tape. Press the flaps in opposite directions. *Figure A*

**5.** Topstitch the hook side of the hook-and-loop tape to the divider pieces, centered between the lines of top stitching on each end. Be sure to place them on opposite sides of the divider piece, as the flaps fold in opposite directions. *Figure B*

## Finishing

**1.** Place the lining into the outer box, wrong sides together. Baste around the top edge with a ¼″ seam allowance.

**2.** Place the unfolded edge of the binding strip along the lining top edge, *right sides together*. Stitch in place with a ⅜″ seam allowance, pivoting at the corners. Join the ends of the binding, by pinning the 2 ends together where they meet evenly. Stitch together and trim off the excess. Press the seam open and finish stitching in place. *Figure C*

**3.** Fold the binding strip over the edge and down toward the outer side and stitch in place near the folded edge. Hand stitching the binding in place may be easiest to manage, due to the size of the completed project, but machine stitching will work as well.

**4.** Measure the grommet placement, marking 2 dots 1½″ down from the top edge and 4″ inward from each corner on each panel with a mesh pocket. Cut out the holes with a small utility knife. Insert grommets, following the manufacturers' instructions. *Figure D*

**5.** Fold over the ends of each 18″ webbing strip ¼″ and zigzag stitch over the raw edges to finish.

**6.** Insert the finished webbing ends through the grommets, from the outside to the inside, and tie a simple knot on each end. *Figure E*

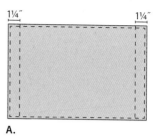

1¼″          1¼″

**A.**

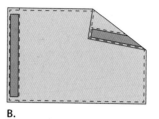

**B.**

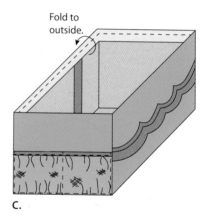

Fold to outside.

**C.**

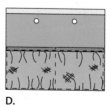

**D.**

**E.**

Made by Janelle MacKay

# Airport Sling

**Finished size:** 9¾″ wide × 11″ long × 1¾″ deep

*Fabric: Tatami from the Bekko Collection by Trenna Travis for Michael Miller, and Beekeeper from the Sweet as Honey Collection by Bonnie Christine for Art Gallery Fabrics*

Traveling back and forth (and back and forth) from Canada to Australia, I've developed a love–hate relationship with airport check-ins. With a young boy tugging on one arm, I needed a really accessible bag to keep my boarding pass and ID from getting lost in a jumbled, heavy backpack. This lightweight, cross-body bag keeps the important stuff in a secure, zippered pocket—perfect if you're chasing down a kid (one last time) or grabbing a pre-flight coffee. Fully lined with an adjustable strap and locking front pocket, this sling is also great for running errands.

**Use it for:**

- Travel documents
- Everyday bag

## PATTERN PIECES

*Refer to Pattern Pieces (page 6).*

- Airport Sling Exterior Panel (pattern pullout page P2)

- Airport Sling Exterior Passport Pocket (pattern pullout page P2)

- Airport Sling Slip Pocket (pattern pullout page P2)

- Airport Sling Slip Pocket Flap (pattern pullout page P2)

## MATERIALS AND SUPPLIES

- **Outer fabric:** ⅝ yard of 54″-wide home decor cotton, sateen, canvas duck, or twill

- **Lining fabric:** ½ yard of 44″-wide quilting cotton

- **Interfacing:** 1 yard of 20″-wide light- to medium-weight, woven, fusible interfacing (such as Pellon Shape-Flex SF101 or Pellon Fusible Featherweight 911FF)

- **Stabilizer:** 2″ × 3″ of one-sided, fusible heavyweight interfacing or stabilizer (such as Pellon Peltex 71F)

- **Purse twist lock**

- **Metal rings for bag strap:** 2, 1″ diameter

- **Metal adjustable slider for bag strap:** 1″

- **Magnetic purse snap:** 9⁄16″ slim

- **Zipper:** 1¼″ wide, heavy duty, 14″ length, #5

- **Water-soluble fabric marker**

- **Double-sided wash-away tape:** ¼″ wide

- **Fray Check**

- **Craft glue:** Clear-drying, fast tack, for metal and fabric

# Cutting

*All cutting measurements are listed as width × height, unless otherwise stated.*

## Outer fabric:

- Cut 1 strip 4¼″ × width of fabric for bag strap.

- Cut 2 strips 2½″ × width of fabric; subcut into 7 strips 10½″ long (4 strips for top and bottom trim on exterior panels, 2 strips for facing pieces on lining panels, and 1 strip for exterior bag base).

- Cut 1 strip 9″ × width of fabric; subcut 2 rectangles 10½″ long for exterior bag panels. Put 1 aside. Fold the other rectangle along the 10½″ side and place the combined exterior panel / slip pocket pattern piece on the fold. Cut on the solid line between the exterior panel and the slip pocket pattern. Do not cut the fold.

> **NOTE**
> If you are using directional fabric, this slip pocket will be cut upside down. Discard this piece and cut 1 more oriented the right direction.

- Cut 1 more slip pocket on fold (2 total).

- Cut 1 exterior passport pocket on fold.

- Cut 2 slip pocket flaps on fold.

- Cut 2 rectangles 4¼″ × 3″ for strap tabs.

- Cut 2 rectangles 1¼″ × 6″ for zipper ends.

## Lining fabric:

- Cut 2 rectangles 10½″ × 10″ for lining side panels.

- Cut 1 rectangle 16″ × 4″ for card slot pocket.

- Cut 2 exterior passport pockets on fold.

- Cut 1 rectangle 2½″ × 10½″ for lining base.

- Cut 1 rectangle 5″ × 7⅛″ for passport pocket lining.

- Cut 1 rectangle 5″ × 2½″ for right side of card slots.

- Cut 1 rectangle 5″ × 1⅝″ for left side of card slots.

## Interfacing:

- Cut 1 rectangle 15½″ × 3½″ for card slot pocket.

- Cut 1 rectangle 4½″ × 6½″ for passport pocket lining.

- Cut 2 slip pocket flaps on fold.

- Cut 2 slip pockets on fold.

- Cut 5 rectangles 2″ × 10″ (2 for exterior base, 1 for lining base, and 2 for lining facing pieces).

## Stabilizer:

- Cut 2 rectangles 2″ × 1½″ for purse lock (1 each for slip pocket flap and slip pocket).

# Instructions

*All seam allowances are ⅜″ unless otherwise noted. (Pocket construction uses a ¼″ seam allowance.)*

**Hint** ▶ Remember to backstitch at the beginning and end of seams. Use a longer stitch length and the appropriate needle for thicker fabrics and top stitching (3–3.5). Topstitching for this project is done in 2 rows: the first is ⅛″ from edge, and the second is ⅛″ from that. Feel free to choose your own top-stitching style.

## Fuse the Interfacing and Stabilizer

**1.** Follow the manufacturer's directions to fuse the interfacing to the *wrong side* of the coordinating pieces. Fuse 2 layers onto the exterior base.

**2.** Round the corners on the 2″ × 1½″ bag stabilizer pieces. Place a piece of stabilizer centered over the marked area on the slip pocket and slip pocket flap per the pattern, for the twist lock to be installed later. Fuse, following the manufacturer's directions. Mark the placement markings on the stabilizer on each piece.

## Assemble Exterior Bag

### Make the Card Slots Pocket

**1.** On the *wrong side* of the 16″ × 4″ rectangle for the card slot pocket, mark the folding lines: Start from the left and mark lines the following widths apart: 2½″ (this is the top), 1¾″, 2¼″, 1¾″, 2¼″, and finally 1¾″. That is 6 lines in total, leaving an extra area at the end of 3¾″. *Figure A*

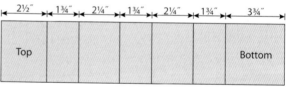

**A.**

**2.** Flip the rectangle over so that it is *right side up*; start folding with right sides together on the first marked line from the left. The next fold will be with the wrong sides together. Press with your iron as you go. This kind of folding is sometimes called *fan folding* or *accordion folding*, and you will alternate the direction of your folds (first to the left, and then to the right). *Figure B*

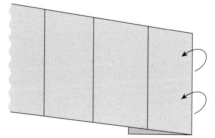

**B.**

**3.** Edgestitch ⅛″ from the folded edge across the tops of the 3 folds that create peaks. *Figure C*

**4.** Refold and pin the sides down so they don't slide. Baste the sides together using a long stitch ⅛″ away from the raw edges. Trim any extra off the bottom of your piece so that it measures 4″ × 5″. *Figure D*

**5.** Using a ¼″ seam allowance, sew the 5″ × 1⅝″ for left side of card slots to the left side edge and the 5″ × 2½″ fabric piece for the right side of card slots to the right side edge. Press seams toward the outer edges.

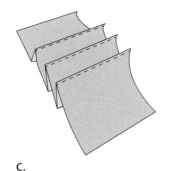

C.

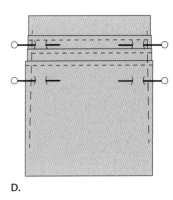

D.

**Hint** The ¼″ seam allowances are very important in this section so that you don't make your card slots too small for your credit cards.

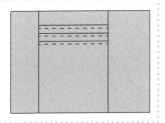

**6.** With *right sides together*, place this piece on top of the 5″ × 7⅛″ passport pocket lining. Using a ¼″ seam allowance, sew across the top edge only.

**7.** Turn *right side out* and press the seam flat. Edgestitch across the top using a ⅛″ seam allowance. *Figure E*

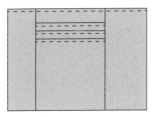

E.

**8.** Place this pocket on an exterior passport pocket lining piece, matching the bottom and side edges. Pin in place. Baste along the sides and bottom, ⅛″ away from raw edges. Create a pen pocket by topstitching, first in the seamline between the 2½″ piece and the card slots, and then back down ⅛″ beside that. *Figure F*

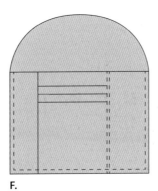

F.

## Tip ←

When installing zippers, zigzag or whipstitch the open ends of the zipper tape closed, just beyond the metal teeth to keep your zipper ends even and easier to manage.

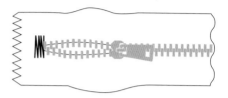

**1.** Press over ¼˝ on each short end of your 6˝-long zipper end strips. Fold these over each end of your zipper, butting the ends up against the metal stops. Using a zipper foot, sew in place using a double row of top stitching. *Figure A*

**2.** Fold the zipper and all exterior passport pocket pieces in half to find the top center of each and mark.

**3.** With the outer fabric pocket *right side up* and the zipper *wrong side up*, align the center mark of the zipper at the top center of exterior passport pocket. Use double-sided tape or pins to keep the zipper in place around the top curve and sides of the pocket.

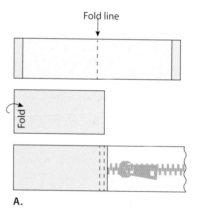

Fold line

Fold

**A.**

**Hint** ▶ Pin at the center and zipper ends and then match the edges in between. Clip the zipper edges if necessary. Make sure your zipper pull is facing down.

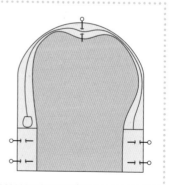

**4.** Place the lining pocket piece *wrong side up* over the top of the exterior and zipper, aligning the edges. Pin or tape all the way around. *Figure B*

**5.** Using a zipper foot, stitch ¼″ away from the edge, sewing the 3 layers together. Turn *right side out* and press.

**6.** Align the top center mark of the other zipper edge to the center mark on the *right side* of the remaining lining piece with the card slot pocket. Use double-sided tape or pins to secure the zipper. Baste the zipper down using a *scant* ¼″ seam. *Figure C*

**7.** Fold the exterior panel to find the center of the inside curve and mark. Clip several tiny notches on the inside curve, making sure you don't clip deeper than ⅛″. With the *right sides together*, secure the inside curve of the exterior panel to the zipper edge on the pocket piece using pins or double-sided tape.

**8.** Using steam and a pressing cloth, press the exterior panel toward the pocket, but press the bottom edges toward the panel. This will reduce the seam thickness and layers in the next step. *Figure D*

**9.** Fold the zipper ends together, *right sides together*, creating a pleat. Pin or clip in place. Baste across the bottom edge of the panel to anchor them down. *Figure E*

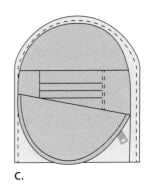

B.

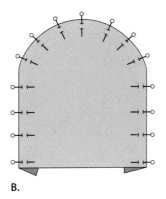

C.

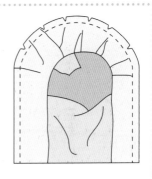

**Hint** First match the center marks and then match and pin down the bottom edges. Stretch the curved edge to the zipper edge, easing in the fullness of the zipper at the curves. Sew through all 3 layers using a ¼″ seam allowance.

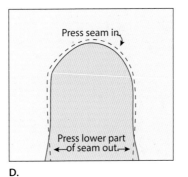

Press seam in
Press lower part of seam out

D.

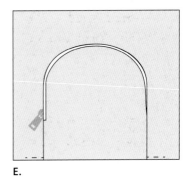

E.

## Make and Attach the Slip Pocket

**1.** Center the washer of the twist lock over the placement mark on the slip pocket, and draw cutting lines for the prongs. *Figure A*

**2.** Using a seam ripper, carefully cut slots slightly smaller than the prongs. Use Fray Check on the holes. Push the twist lock in from the right side of the slip pocket, place the provided washer over the back, and use a screwdriver to bend the prongs tightly down onto the washer so that they are facing inward. *Figure B*

A.

B.

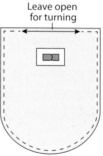

Leave open for turning

C.

## Tip

**Cut a piece of fusible fleece, felt, or interfacing larger than the washer plate. Fuse or glue this over the washer and prongs to prevent the metal from wearing through your fabric or damaging anything placed in your pocket.**

**3.** Place the 2 slip pocket pieces *right sides together* and pin around the edges. Sew a ¼″ seam around all the edges, but leave an opening for turning on the top straight edge.

**4.** Clip the corners and trim the seam allowance to ⅛″. *Figure C*

**5.** Turn the pocket *right side out*, push out the corners, and press the opening to the inside.

**6.** Topstitch 2 lines across the straight edge of the pocket only, closing the opening as you go. *Figure D*

**7.** Repeat Steps 3–5 for the slip pocket flap.

D.

**8.** Topstitch around the curved edge of the pocket flap, leaving the top open. Fold the top edge in ¼" and press. Pin the opening closed. *Figure E*

**E.**

**9.** Use the marking on the slip pocket flap pattern to mark the placement for the front and back plates of the twist lock. Trace the holes on the back plate onto the flap, snip the holes, and attach the back plate using the manufacturer's directions. *Figure F*

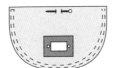

**F.**

**10.** Place the flap onto the slip pocket, closing the lock, and center this pocket unit on the other 10½" wide × 10" high exterior panel. Measure for the center and pin the slip pocket in place.

**11.** Undo the lock and remove the flap piece. Topstitch around the side and bottom edges of the pocket, leaving the top open.

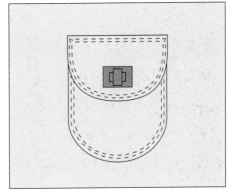

**12.** Replace the slip pocket flap and pin it back in place. Topstitch across the top only, anchoring it in place. *Figure G*

**G.**

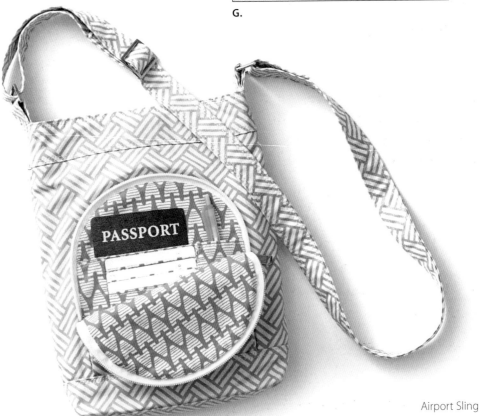

### Assemble the Exterior Shell

**1.** Place 1 top exterior trim piece and 1 bottom trim piece right sides together onto one exterior panel. Sew the seam, press toward the trim, and topstitch on the trim side of the seam. Repeat for the second exterior panel. *Figure A*

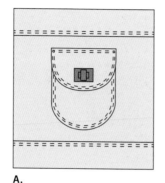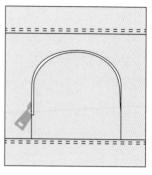

A.

**2.** Find and mark the center of the bottom of both exterior panels and the long sides of the exterior bag base. Match the centers and pin a panel to each side of the base. Sew and press the seams toward the center. Topstitch the seams on the side of the bag base. *Figure B*

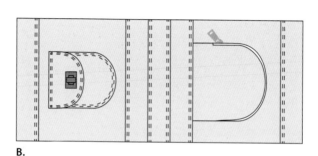

B.

**3.** With *right sides together*, pin and sew the side seams, folding the bag base in half as needed. Press the side seams open. *Figure C*

**4.** Clip the seam allowance on the exterior panel at the corner point so that it will open; lay the open side, seam down, onto the bag base, creating a point. Make sure the seam is centered on the base, press, and pin in place. *Figure D*

C.

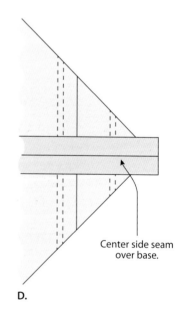

Center side seam over base.

D.

**5.** Turn the bag over so you can see the base. Double-check the centering and place the ruler at point of the corner that measures 1¾". Draw a line across the triangle at the 1¾" mark. *Figure E*

**6.** Stitch across this line a couple times to secure, and again ⅛" next to it. Trim off the corner. Repeat for the other side. Turn the bag exterior right side out. *Figure F*

## Make the Strap and Tabs

**1.** Refer to 4-Fold Open-End Strap (page 10) to create 2 small straps from the 2 strap tab rectangles.

> **NOTE**
> The 4¼" measurement is the width and the 3" measurement is the length.

**2.** Topstitch the open side of the strap tab first, then across the bottom and back up the other side. Repeat to make 2 rows of topstitching to match the rest of your bag.

**3.** Slide a 1" metal ring onto each strap tab and baste the ends closed using a ⅛" seam allowance.

**4.** Center the strap tabs on the right side of the exterior bag side seams, matching raw edges, and pin to secure. Baste the strap tabs in place using a ¼" seam allowance. *Figure G*

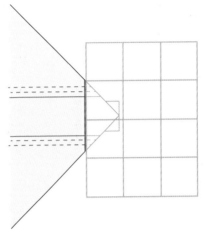

E.

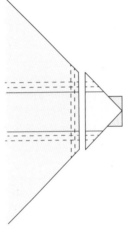

F.

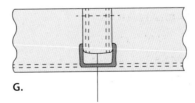

G.

## Assemble the Lining

**1.** Measure and mark the exact center on the *wrong side* of lining facing pieces cut from exterior fabric. Attach 1 magnetic snap (page 13). Attach the male magnetic snap side to 1 lining top piece and the female snap side to the other. *Figure A*

**2.** Sew 1 facing piece to the top of each lining panel, right sides together. Press the seams toward the bottom panel and topstitch on the lining side of the seam. Repeat Assemble the Exterior Shell, Steps 2–6 (page 118), except leave a 5″ opening for turning on one side. Leave lining *wrong side out. Figure B*

## Attach the Exterior to the Lining

**1.** With the lining *wrong side out* and the bag exterior *right side out*, slide the bag exterior into the lining. Match the side seams and centers and pin around the bag opening. *Figure C*

**2.** Using a ⅜″ seam allowance, sew around the bag opening. Turn the bag *right side out* using the turning hole in the lining. Sew the lining hole closed by machine with a ¹⁄₁₆″ seam allowance, or use an invisible slip stitch by hand. Push the lining down inside the bag exterior.

**3.** Press the seam around the bag opening. Topstitch around the bag opening.

## Add the Adjustable Strap

**1.** Refer to 4-Fold Closed-End strap (page 11) to create 1 long strap from the bag strap piece. Topstitch in the same style as you did for the strap tabs.

**2.** Refer to Adjustable Strap (page 12) to attach your strap to the strap tab rings.

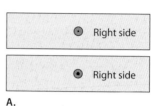

A.

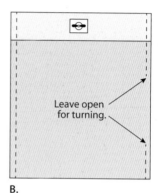

Leave open for turning.

B.

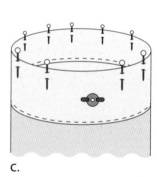

C.

Made by Jennie Pickett and Clara Jung

# Snap-and-Go
# Sewing or Art Case

**Finished size:** 14″ × 12½″ × 1″

*Fabrics: Mustang by Melody Miller and Netorious, Cotton + Steel*

When sewing on the go, I like to have a clear view of all my supplies so I don't have to go digging through a bag. The large vinyl pocket of this craft organizer stows an embroidery hoop or even a small cutting mat, while the clear zippered pockets are perfect for organizing tools and notions. Two snap-off pockets keep small projects and supplies. If you use one set of snaps on the panels and a second set of snaps on the pouches, you can easily make extra pouches to swap in and out, in case you have more than two projects in the queue.

### Use it for:

- Sewing supplies for travel
- Sketchbook and art supplies
- Jewelry
- Kids' road-trip games and activities

## PATTERN PIECES

*Refer to Pattern Pieces (page 6).*

- Corner (pattern pullout page P2) *(Refer to Curved Corners, page 7.)*

## MATERIALS AND SUPPLIES

- **Main fabrics:** 4 fat quarters (18″ × 22″)
- **Lining and handle fabric:** ⅝ yard
- **Binding fabric:** ⅝ yard
- **Interfacing:** 1 yard of 20″-wide light- to medium-weight, woven, fusible interfacing (such as Pellon Shape-Flex SF101 or Fusible Midweight 931TD)
- **Stabilizer:** ½ yard of one-sided fusible fleece (such as Pellon 987F)
- **Zippers:** 4, 12″ length
- **Bag zipper with 2 pulls:** 40″ length
- **Plastic snaps:** 6 pairs
- **Snap pliers**
- **Clear vinyl:** 8 gauge, ½ yard

# Cutting

*All cutting measurements are listed as width × height, unless otherwise stated.*

## From each fat quarter 1 and 2 (pink flowers and navy arrows):

- Cut 2 rectangles 3½″ × 14″ for patchwork outer.

- Cut 1 rectangle 2⅛″ × 12½″ for zipper panel.

- Cut 1 rectangle 3″ × 9″ for pouch snap panel.

- Cut 1 rectangle 2″ × 11″ for pouch front.

- Cut 1 rectangle 2⅝″ × 11″ for pouch back.

## Fat quarter 3 (mustangs):

- Cut 2 rectangles 3½″ × 14″ for patchwork outer.

- Cut 1 rectangle 3½″ × 12″ for zipper panel.

## Fat quarter 4 (stars):

- Cut 2 rectangles 3½″ × 14″ for patchwork outer.

- Cut 2 rectangles 3½″ × 9″ for bag snap panels.

## Lining fabric (salmon arrows):

- Cut 2 rectangles 12½″ × 14″ for bag lining.

- Cut 2 strips 5″ × 13½″ for handles.

- Cut 2 rectangles 2″ × 2¾″ for zipper tabs.

## Binding fabric:

*Note: The following strips do not need to be cut on the bias.*

- Cut 3 strips 3″ wide for the perimeter double-layer binding.

- Cut 4 strips 1⅞″ wide for the interior double-fold binding.

## Vinyl:

- Cut 1 rectangle 12″ × 12½″ for large pocket.

- Cut 1 rectangle 4″ × 12½″ for lower zipper panel.

- Cut 1 rectangle 3″ × 12½″ for upper zipper panel.

- Cut 2 rectangles 11″ × 15″ for pouches.

## Interfacing:

- Cut 2 rectangles 12½″ × 14″ for bag lining.

- Cut 2 rectangles 3″ × 9″ for pouch snap panels.

- Cut 2 rectangles 3½″ × 9″ for bag snap panels.

## Stabilizer:

- Cut 1 rectangle 14″ × 24½″ for bag body.

# Instructions

*All seam allowances are ¼". I recommend the use of binding clips rather than pins when working with vinyl to avoid making permanent holes. Also, to avoid perforating the vinyl, use a slightly longer stitch length than normal.*

## Sew the Patchwork Outer

**1.** With *right sides together*, sew together the long sides of the 8 rectangles 3½" × 14" to create the patchwork outer.

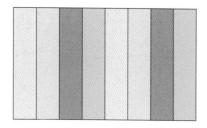

**2.** Press all the seams open.

## Fuse the Interfacing and Stabilizer

**1.** Follow the manufacturer's directions to fuse interfacing to the *wrong side* of the 2 largest lining pieces. Fuse interfacing to the *wrong side* of 2 snap panels for the bag and 2 snap panels for the pouches.

**2.** Follow the manufacturer's directions to fuse the stabilizer to the *wrong side* of the patchwork bag outer.

## Make Binding

**1.** To make the binding for the perimeter of the bag, join the 3" bias strips end-to-end with ¼" seams. Press the seams open and then fold and press the strip in half lengthwise.

**2.** To make the double-fold binding for the interior, join the 1⅞" strips end to end with ¼" seams and press the seams open. Fold and press the strip in the same manner as 4-Fold Open-End Strap (page 10).

## Quilt the Bag Outer

Sew ⅛" and ¼" away from each seamline to quilt the bag outer to the fusible fleece.

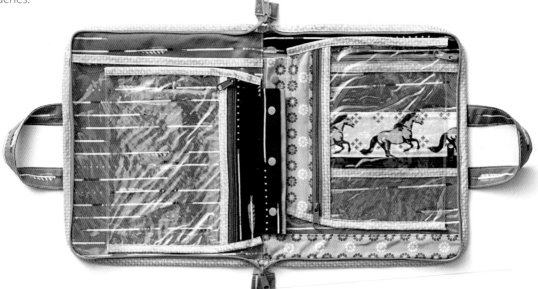

## Make the Large Vinyl Pocket

**1.** Sew a 12½˝ length of double-fold binding to the top of the short edge of the large vinyl pocket piece by slipping the vinyl into the fold of the double-fold binding and stitching close to the inner fold, catching the bottom layer as well.

**2.** Position the vinyl pocket on the bottom edge of 1 bag lining piece and stitch in place *with a ⅛˝ seam allowance* along the sides and bottom edges. *Figure A*

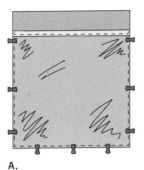

A.

## Make the Zipper Panel

**1.** Assemble the zipper panel from the bottom up, beginning with the zipper panel piece from fat quarter 1.

**2.** Use the following method to sew fabric to vinyl, vinyl to zipper, and zipper to fabric.

B.

### Sew Fabric to Vinyl

**1.** Use the zipper panel piece from fat quarter 1 and fold ¼˝ over, *wrong sides together*, on one long edge. Press.

**2.** Place the 4˝ zipper panel vinyl rectangle over the *right side* of the fabric piece, aligning the top edge with the folded edge. Stitch through the vinyl and fabric. *Figure B*

**3.** Fold the fabric at the seam to enclose the raw edge of the fabric. Topstitch through the fabric and vinyl to finish the seam. *Figure C*

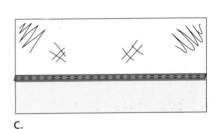

C.

### Sew Zipper to Vinyl

**1.** Sew a 12½˝ length of double-fold binding to the opposite long edge of the vinyl by slipping the vinyl into the fold of the binding and stitching close to the inner fold, catching the bottom layer as well.

**2.** Place the zipper behind the binding. Use a zipper foot to sew the zipper to the binding. *Figure D*

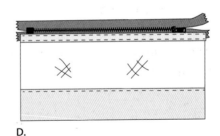

D.

### Sew Fabric to Zipper

**1.** Place the fat quarter 3 zipper panel piece and zipper *right sides together*, so that the raw edge of the fabric does not extend past the zipper tape. Use the zipper foot to sew along the edge.

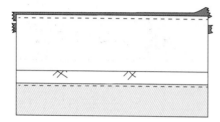

**2.** Fold the fabric at the seam to enclose the raw edge with the zipper tape; topstitch through the zipper and fabric to finish the seam.

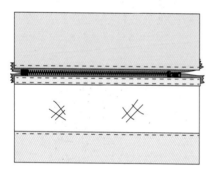

### Finish Zipper Panel

**1.** Repeat the methods to attach the remaining zipper panel vinyl, zipper, and fat quarter 2 piece to complete the zipper panel.

**2.** Place the zipper panel on top of the *right side* of the second lining piece. Sew the zipper panel in place on all 4 sides *with a ⅛″ seam allowance.*

**3.** Topstitch through the zipper panel and the lining piece across the center of the fat quarter 3 piece to divide the pockets.

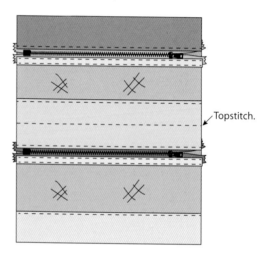

Topstitch.

## Make the Bag Snap Panels

**1.** Fold 1 bag snap panel piece in half lengthwise, *right sides together*, and sew along the 2 short edges. Clip the corners nearest the fold.

**2.** Turn *right side out* and press. Measure ¾″ down from the folded edge of the snap panel and mark the center point and 1¼″ from each short edge. Follow manufacturer's directions to apply one-half of 3 snap pairs to the snap panel. Repeat with the second bag snap panel piece. Reserve the second half of the snap pairs for the pouch snap panels.

## Assemble Bag Lining

**1.** Position 1 snap panel along the left edge 2″ from the top of the zipper panel lining piece edge. Then position the other snap panel 2″ below the top of the first panel. Place the large pocket lining piece with the vinyl pocket *right side down* on top of the zipper panel and snap panels. Sew along the snap panel edge.

**2.** Finger press the seam allowance toward the large pocket lining piece. Topstitch ⅛″ from the edge of the large pocket lining piece to keep the seam allowance in place. *Figure A*

## Make the Handles

**1.** Fold ¼″ of each short edge of the handle piece toward the *wrong side*. Refer to 4-Fold Closed-End Strap (page 11) to make the handles.

**2.** Pin the handles on each end of the bag outer placing each handle end 4½″ from the sides and 1¼″ above the patchwork seamline. Sew a rectangle with an X on each handle end to secure in place. *Figure B*

## Assemble the Bag

**1.** Layer the bag body and lining *wrong sides together* and stitch ⅛″ around the edge to baste together. Use the 2″ marking on the Corner Template to trim all 4 corners.

**2.** Refer to Attaching Bias Binding, Steps 1–4 (page 16), to sew the double-layer binding around the perimeter of exterior of the bag, but do not complete Steps 5 and 6 to sew the binding down to the lining side yet. *Figure C*

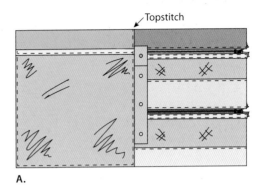

Topstitch

**A.**

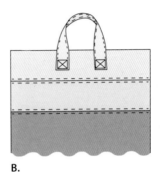

**B.**

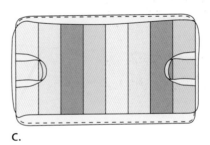

**C.**

## Attach the Long Zipper

**1.** Fold the binding around to the *inside* of the organizer, enclosing the raw edges of the outer perimeter, referring to Attaching Bias Binding, Steps 5 and 6 (page 17). Unzip the zipper all the way and position the zipper, *right side up*, around the edge of the bag. Place the zipper tape underneath the binding edge. The zipper pulls should be positioned at the center seam of the organizer. Use clips to hold the zipper in place under the binding.

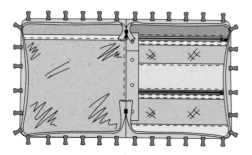

**2.** Turn the organizer over and stitch *right next to* the edge of the binding, through the zipper, securing the inside edge of the binding and zipper to the edge of the bag.

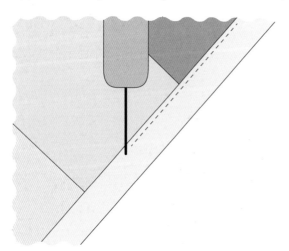

**1.** Fold ¼″ on each short edge of the zipper tabs to the wrong side. Fold in half, *right sides together*, with the folded edges touching, and stitch ¼″ on each short edge. Clip the corners nearest the crosswise fold. Turn *right side out*.

**2.** Unzip the zipper so the bag lies flat. Mark the end of the zipper 1¼″ past the zipper pull and stitch the zipper tape closed with a zigzag stitch, then trim the zipper. Stitch together and trim the other end of the zipper in the same manner. Slip the zipper tabs over each end of the zipper and sew in place. The zipper tabs can be tucked inside or left outside the case.

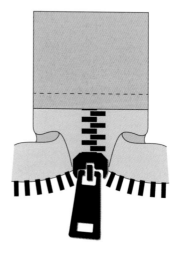

## Make the Removable Pouches

**1.** Use the same methods in Make the Zipper Panel (page 125) to make the removable pouches. Attach the 2⅝″ × 11″ pouch piece to one short edge of the pouch vinyl. Attach the zipper to the opposite short edge of the vinyl with the double-fold binding. Then attach the 2″ × 11″ pouch piece to the zipper. *Figure A*

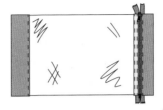

**A.**

**2.** Make the pouch snap panel in the same way as Make the Bag Snap Panels (page 126). Mark identical snap locations ½″ from the folded edge. Follow the manufacturer's directions to apply the second half of the snap pairs remaining from the bag snap panels. *Figure B*

**B.**

**3.** Fold the pouch with the fabrics *right sides together* and the snap panel between the fabric ends of the pouch, edges aligned. Stitch along the long edge of the fabric and snap panel edge. Turn the pouch *right side out. Figure C*

**C.**

**4.** Topstitch ⅜″ from the seam, along the top edge of the pouch.

**5.** Measure ½″ out from the edge of the snap panel and mark. Draw an angled line from the mark to the edge of the vinyl and trim the pouch. Repeat for the other edge. *Figure D*

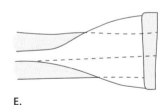

Vinyl Pocket

**D.**                        **E.**

**6.** Cut 2 lengths of double-fold binding ½″ longer than the pouch open edges. Unfold the binding and on each end fold ¼″ toward the *wrong side* of the binding and press. Then fold the binding as before. *Figure E*

**7.** Apply binding to the unfinished sides of the pouch in the same manner as in Sew Zipper to Vinyl, Step 1 (page 125). *Figure F*

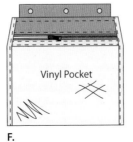

Vinyl Pocket

**F.**

**8.** Repeat to make a second removable pouch.

# Air-It-Out Gym Tote

Made by Lorraine Teigland

**Finished size:** 10″ (diameter) × 20″ (shoulder strap adjusts between 17″ and 31″)

*Fabric: Outdoor canvas from JoAnn Fabrics*

The Air-It-Out Gym Tote is a sturdy carryall for trips to the gym, the pool, or a sports game. Its partial-mesh construction and ripstop nylon lining allow ventilation of its contents and easy cleaning of its interior and make it perfect for toting all kinds of sports gear. An inside pocket organizes personal items like gym membership cards, keys, and cash. The tote rests comfortably over the shoulder with its adjustable strap and handle, and it hangs from wall and door hooks when not in use.

**Use it for:**

- Swimming gear
- Workout clothes and shoes
- Sports equipment

## MATERIALS AND SUPPLIES

- **Outer fabric:** ¾ yard of 54″-wide home decor weight or heavier

- **Lining fabric (ripstop nylon):** ⅜ yard

- **Mesh fabric (pet screening):** ¾ yard

- **Binding trim or ribbon:** ½″ or ⅝″ wide, ¾ yard

- **Piping cord:** ¼″ or ⅜″ wide, 1 yard

- **Webbing:** 2″ wide, 1½ yards

- **Rectangular loop and slide buckle set:** 2″ plastic

- **Drawstring cord:** ¼″ or ⅜″ wide, 50″ length

- **Cord stop:** to fit drawstring cord

- **Grommets:** 8 at ⁷⁄₁₆″ wide

- **Regular presser foot and zipper foot**

- **Denim/jeans needle and universal needle**

- **Removable tape or marker**

# Cutting

## Outer fabric:

- Cut 1 rectangle 9½″ × 32½″ for bottom band.

- Cut 1 circle 11″ diameter for base.

- Cut 2 strips 4″ × 32½″ for upper bands.

- Cut 1 strip 2″ × 34″ for piping (or substitute alternate fabric for contrast).

- Cut 1 rectangle 9″ × 8″ for pocket.

## Lining fabric:

- Cut 1 rectangle 9½″ × 32½″ for bottom band.

- Cut 1 circle 11″ diameter for base.

- Cut 1 rectangle 9″ × 8″ for pocket.

## Mesh fabric:

- Cut 1 rectangle 20″ × 32½″ for side panel.

## Webbing:

- Cut 1 piece 36″ long for strap.

- Cut 1 piece 6″ long for strap anchor.

- Cut 1 piece 10″ long for handle.

# Instructions

*All seam allowances are ½″ initially; they may be trimmed in later stages.*

**Hint** > This entire project can be sewn with a universal needle. However, if using canvas fabrics, better top-stitching results are achieved with a denim needle. A sewing machine with a free arm will make it easier to work with the stiff mesh fabric in this project.

## Make the Pocket

**1.** Lay the 9″ × 8″ outer and lining fabric pocket pieces with their *right sides together* and sew all around, leaving a 3″ section open on one of the 9″ sides for turning out. *Figure A*

**2.** Clip the corners, turn right side out through the opening, and press the seams.

**3.** Topstitch a rectangle 1″ wide close to the 9″ edge with the opening, sewing the opening shut in the process. This is the top edge of the pocket. *Figure B*

**4.** Center the pocket on the *right side* of the lining fabric bottom band with the outside fabric side of the pocket facing out. Sew around the sides and bottom edge of the pocket to attach. *Figure C*

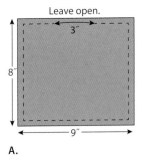

Leave open.

8″

9″

**A.**

**B.**

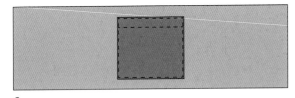

**C.**

## Assemble the Inner Base

**1.** Line up the short sides of the 9½″ × 32½″ lining fabric bottom band with *right sides together* and sew this seam to make a wide cylinder. Fold both seam allowances to one side. *Figure A*

**2.** Working with the cylinder *wrong side out*, topstitch on the *right side* of the seam, through the seam allowances, to reinforce the seam.

**3.** Make ¼″-deep snips ½″ apart in the seam allowance along the bottom edge of the cylinder. *Figure B*

**4.** Make quarter marks along this same bottom edge and around the circumference of the 11″ lining fabric base. With *right sides together*, match up these quarter marks, pinning in place if necessary. *Figure C*

**5.** With the circle base below and the cylinder bottom band above, sew around the lower edge of the cylinder to attach it to the circle, spreading the snipped seam allowance around the circumference of the circle to fit. *Figure D*

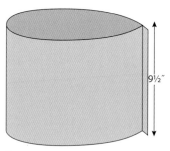

9½″

**A.**

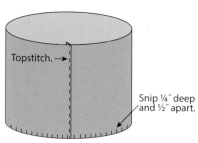

Topstitch. →

Snip ¼″ deep and ½″ apart.

**B.**

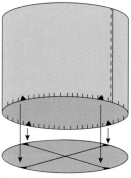

**C.**

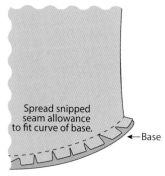

Spread snipped seam allowance to fit curve of base.

←Base

**D.**

## Assemble the Outer Base

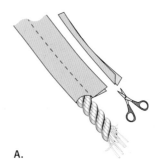

**A.**

**1.** With *right sides facing out*, fold the 2″ × 34″ strip of outer fabric for piping lengthwise along its midline over the piping cord to enclose it snugly against the fold line. Using the zipper foot and with the needle in the side position, sew long basting stitches close to the piping cord to hold it in place. This is the first line of stitching. Trim the seam allowance to ½″ if necessary. Refer to Piping (page 18). *Figure A*

**2.** With *right sides together*, sew the short sides of the 9½″ × 32½″ outer fabric bottom band together. Fold the seam to one side and topstitch on the *right side* of the seam as you did with the lining fabric rectangle.

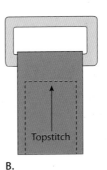

Topstitch

**B.**

**3.** Insert the 6″ strip of webbing through the plastic rectangular loop, bring the 2 ends together, and topstitch an open rectangle through both layers, as close to the loop as possible, to hold the loop in place. This is the strap anchor. *Figure B*

**4.** Lay the strap anchor centered along the seamline on the *right side* of the outer fabric cylinder. Line up the short edge of the strap anchor with the seam allowance of the cylinder and sew within the seam allowance to attach. *Figure C*

**C.**

**5.** Lay the piping on the *right side* of the cylinder, lining up the seam allowances. Using the zipper foot, begin sewing about 1″ from the head end of the piping to attach it to the lower edge of the cylinder. This is the second line of stitching, so it should be just inside the first line, closer to the cord. *Figure D*

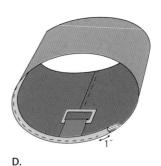

1″

**D.**

**6.** After sewing almost all the way around the circle, stop at about 1½″ from the head end, leaving the needle in the down position. Unpick the remaining stitches along the tail end of the piping strip and open it up. Snip off the tail end of the cord so that it just meets the head end of the cord without overlapping. Trim the piping fabric 1″ beyond the cord. *Figure E*

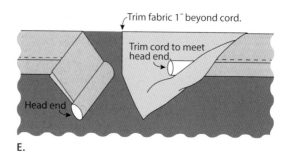

Trim fabric 1″ beyond cord.

Trim cord to meet head end.

Head end

**E.**

**7.** Fold in about ½″ of the tail end of the piping fabric, insert the head end of the piping, and refold the fabric shut over the meeting cord ends. Resume sewing to complete the circle, securing the piping junction. *Figure F*

**8.** Repeat Steps 3–5 of Assemble the Inner Base (page 134) to attach the 11″ outer fabric circle base to the bottom piped edge of the outer fabric cylinder. Use the zipper foot to help you sew this third line of stitching as close to the piping cord as you can.

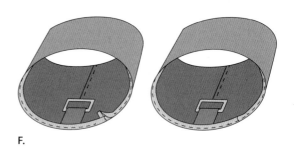

**F.**

## Attach the Base Cylinders

**1.** Sew the short sides of the mesh fabric side panel together to make a tall cylinder. There is no right side or wrong side to the mesh fabric; however, the side with the seam allowance is hereafter the *wrong side*. Trim the seam allowance to ¼″ and bind the raw edge with the trim or ribbon. Cut off any trim or ribbon that protrudes beyond the seam. Leave the cylinder wrong side out.

**2.** From one end (hereafter called the bottom end), mark off 9″ distances all around the cylinder with tape or marker. Fold or roll the other end of the cylinder to about 5″ from the marked line. This is to reduce bulk under the machine arm while sewing. Flip the mesh cylinder upside down so the bottom end is pointing up. *Figure G*

**3.** With the mesh cylinder *wrong side out*, insert the outer base cylinder (*right side out*, base down) *into* the mesh cylinder. Line up the side seams. Place the top edge of the outer cylinder exactly with the 9″ line you marked earlier. Pin temporarily in place.

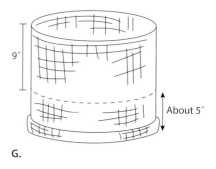

9″

About 5″

**G.**

**4.** Insert this mesh cylinder unit *into* the inner base cylinder (*wrong side out*, base down). Match up the midline of the pocket with the seamline of the mesh cylinder. Place the top edge of the inner base cylinder exactly with the 9″ line. Pin through all 3 layers to hold them in place. Check that the *right sides* of both base cylinders are touching the mesh fabric. The top edges and the 9″ line on the mesh are red in the illustration. *Figure H*

**5.** Sew all around the top edge of the outer and inner base cylinders, through all 3 layers, leaving a 7″ section open (unstitched) for turning out. Remember to backstitch! *Figure I*

**6.** Remove all pins and carefully turn all fabrics out through the opening until the mesh cylinder itself is *right side out*. Carefully press (with finger or cool iron) the fold along which the inner and outer fabric base cylinders attach to the mesh cylinder. Edgestitch along the fold, closing the openings on both sides in the process. *Figure J*

## Make and Attach the Shoulder Strap

**1.** Loop one end of the 36″ strip of webbing through the center bar of the slide buckle, tuck in a ⅜″ hem, and topstitch a rectangle to secure. *Figure K*

**2.** Loop the other end through the rectangular loop on the outer base cylinder, and then through the buckle, as shown. *Figure L*

**3.** Position the loose end centrally along the seam of the mesh cylinder, 2″ from the top edge. Sew in place. *Figure M*

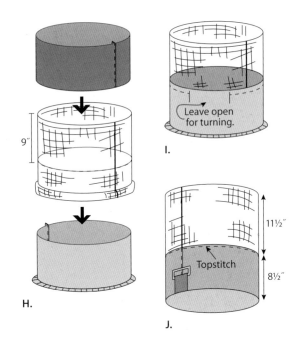

H.

I. Leave open for turning.

J. 11½″ Topstitch 8½″

9″

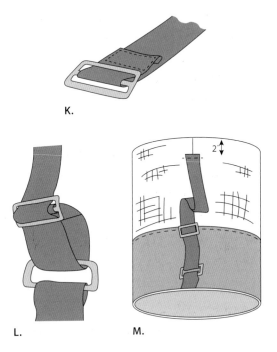

K.

L.

M. 2″

## Attach the Upper Bands

**1.** With *right sides together*, sew together the short sides of 1 strip of 4″ × 32½″ outer fabric for upper bands to make a short and wide cylinder. Press the seam to one side. Press the ½″ seam allowance of one long edge to the *wrong side* and topstitch on the *right side* of the side seam, through the seam allowances, to hold the seam allowance in place.

**2.** Repeat Step 1 with the other strip of fabric to make and prepare a second identical cylinder. These are the upper bands.

**3.** From the top edge of the mesh cylinder, measure and mark 2½″ distances all around.

**4.** Work with the mesh cylinder *right side out*. Insert 1 upper band, *right side out, inside* the opening of the mesh cylinder with the side seam across the circle from the seam of the mesh fabric. Line up the unpressed edge exactly with the 2½″ line and with the pressed edge pointing toward the interior of the tote. Pin temporarily in place.

**5.** Slide the second upper band, *wrong side out*, over the *outside* of the mesh cylinder so that its unpressed edge lines up exactly with the 2½″ line and the pressed edge is pointing down. Adjust the alignment so that the seam of this outer band lines up with the seam of the mesh fabric. Pin through all 3 layers. Check that the *right sides* of both upper bands are touching the mesh fabric. *Figure A*

**6.** Sew along the unpressed edges of the upper bands, through all 3 layers, securing and enclosing the top edge of the shoulder strap in the process. Sew all around the circumference and do not leave an opening. Remove all pins and press the seam (using a finger or cool iron).

**7.** Flip both upper bands up so their pressed edges meet over the top edge of the mesh cylinder. If necessary, trim the top edge of the mesh fabric to tuck completely into the seam allowance of 1 upper band. Edge stitch along the top and bottom folded edges of the upper bands, through all layers. *Figure B*

**8.** At the attachment site of the top of the shoulder strap, sew a rectangle through all layers to reinforce the site. *Figure C*

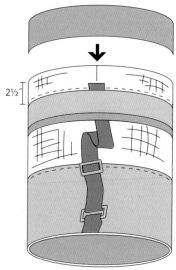

**A.**

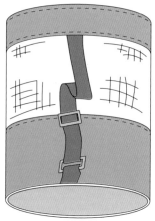

**B.**

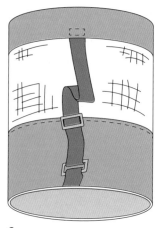

**C.**

## Attach the Handle

**1.** Measure and mark 3¼″ on either side of the seam of the outside upper band. *Figure D*

**2.** Fold in ½″ on each end of the 10″ webbing handle. Position the folded ends of the handle at each of the 3¼″ marks with the seam allowance tucked between the handle and the bag. Sew rectangles about ¾″ wide to secure and reinforce the folded ends of the handle to the bag. *Figure E*

## Install the Grommets and Drawstring Cord

**1.** Using the manufacturer's instructions, install the 8 grommets along the upper band, equidistant from the top and bottom edges, as follows:

Install 2 grommets as far apart as possible (approximately 3½″) *under* the handle (between the 2 sewn ends of the handle).

Evenly space (approximately 3½″ apart) the other 6 grommets along the remaining portion of the upper band.

**2.** Thread the drawstring cord through the grommets so the ends emerge from the frontmost 2 grommets (opposite the handle). Thread the ends through the cord stop. Knot the ends together to prevent them from slipping out of the cord stop.

## Variations

**1.** For a simpler construction, omit the piping.

**2.** Ripstop lining is used for applications involving wet or dirty gear, as it is easy to wipe clean. Similarly, the mesh fabric allows ventilation of the bag contents for quick drying and odor control. These fabrics can easily be substituted with other fabrics such as canvas, vinyl or cotton (with appropriate interfacing) for different uses.

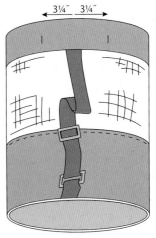

D.

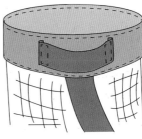

E.

# Meet the

**Sara Curtis** is a wife and mother of six curious and lively children. When she was a child, her parents often took spontaneous road trips, cultivating her passion for beauty and adventure. She shares her passions through writing, sewing, and designing. Though her first priority is teaching her children, Sara enjoys being able to teach

Photo by Sara Curtis

others how to sew through her blog and sewing patterns. Her patterns have been featured in *Stitch* magazine, and on numerous websites including *Sew Mama Sew* and *Spoonflower*. Sara and her husband have moved their family all over the country, but they currently live and work in North Carolina. You can find more of Sara's creative work on her blog, *Radiant Home Studio*. **radianthomestudio.com**

**Rachael Gander** is a sewist, mom, wife, designer, blogger, and fabric enthusiast who learned to sew alongside her mom but lost interest in the craft until she was in her early 20s. She has spent the last 15 years making up for lost time, experimenting with modern quilting, accessory and garment sewing, hand-printed fabric, and textile

Photo by Marissa Bower

design. Along with documenting her creative journey on her blog, Imagine Gnats, Rachael sells her original sewing and embroidery patterns in the Imagine Gnats shop. *imaginegnats.com*

**Samantha Hussey**, a.k.a. Mrs. H, is a sewing pattern designer living in the lush green valleys of Wales in the UK, with her "Dusband" Mr. H and their baby daughter, unfortunately nicknamed Elvis. Samantha learned to sew at school but didn't start professionally until 2010, when inspiration struck, prompting her to think

Photo by Jonathan Hussey

up creative solutions to making difficult bags easier to sew. Since then, she's launched a range of sewing patterns for all skill abilities and blogs about her slightly random home life. This is all done while she's supposed to be working for the family website coding business. She spends far more time sewing than working—just don't tell her boss, Mr. H! To see the full range of patterns, visit *mrs-h.co.uk*.

# Designers ←──────

**Mary Jaracz** lives in the Midwest with her awesome husband, Kyle, and their two fun and crazy little

boys. They're slowly updating and renovating their historic home, which was built in the late 1800s. Their boys work hard at destroying the house faster than it can be repaired. Mary was a full-time graphic designer who switched to freelance graphic design work after becoming a stay-at-home mom. She first learned to sew as a child. After college, she started sewing again and hasn't stopped since! She blogs with Lindsay Conner about tutorials, contests, and other sewing- and crafting-related fun at *Craft Buds*. ***craftbuds.com***

**Sara Lawson** started her sewing blog, *Sew Sweetness*, in September 2010. Since then, she has

written bag patterns for Pellon, for magazines, and for her own pattern line. She is the author of two bag books and has designed two lines of fabric for Art Gallery Fabrics. She lives in Chicago with her husband and two children. ***sewsweetness.com***

**Veronica Lovvorn** grew up in the Deep South, where she learned to sew by helping her mother

and grandmother cut out fabric and sew pretty clothes for her. Later, Veronica spent more than a decade as an engineer in airport design/planning until she retired her briefcase and resurrected her mom's vintage Bernina sewing machine to sew outfits for her own daughter, Ella. Soon after, she started the blog, *sewVery*, to chronicle her sewing creations. Now Veronica rarely goes a day without sewing and blogging about a piece of children's clothing or a handbag she has made! Most recently, Veronica began using her designing and drafting skills again to create children's clothing patterns that she sells in her sewVery pattern shop. ***sewvery.blogspot.com***

**Jennie Pickett and Clara Jung** are a mother–daughter team who work together, long-distance,  designing patchwork bag patterns. In 2009 they started Clover & Violet, LLC, and their handmade business quickly evolved into a bag-pattern design company. Their bag designs seek to blend pretty patchwork with useful features that are tailored toward specific purposes. Jennie lives in New York with her husband and three children, finding time to sew and design during naptime. Clara lives in Virginia with her husband, sewing and designing when they're not traveling the country. Clover & Violet patterns have been featured in kits by RJR Fabrics and published in *American Quilter Magazine*. Jennie and Clara share their new designs and other creative endeavors at **cloverandviolet.com**.

**Lorraine Teigland** is a retired high school physics teacher who now stays home with her three  daughters, ages 6, 8, and 10. As a child growing up in Singapore, she learned to sew from her mother, aunt, and grandmother, who was a tailor. She sews garments, toys, bags, and other random items. When she needs a break from sewing, she makes things from corrugated cardboard and wood, and eats Nutella. She is married to a software engineer, whose sense of reality and humor have saved her from attempting, and failing at, some very daft crafts. Many of the things she creates are inspired by watching her girls at play. Someday, she would like her children to enjoy sewing even more than she does and be better at it than she ever was. **ikatbag.com**

**Michelle Webster** writes and sells a popular line of PDF accessory sewing patterns. She lives in  Portland, Oregon, and appreciates the creative atmosphere of the city, as well the lush and green natural setting. When she's not sewing accessories, you might find her embroidering, dabbling in quilting, or making the occasional piece of clothing. You can see Michelle's full pattern line at **michellepatterns.com**.

# About the Authors

*Photo by Jeremiah Blackford*

**Lindsay Conner** is a writer, editor, and quilter living in Nashville, Tennessee, with her husband, their baby boy, and two lovable cats. In 2011, Lindsay and her crafty partner-in-crime Mary Jaracz launched the blog *Craft Buds*, a space to share handmade business tips and tutorials. She is the author of *Modern Bee—13 Quilts to Make with Friends*, and her designs have appeared in many books and magazines. When she's not sewing, Lindsay keeps busy as an ambassador for Baby Lock sewing machines, a writer for the Craftsy quilting blog, and a pattern designer for Pellon and several fabric companies. She blogs about her crafty ventures at *Lindsay Sews*. **lindsaysews.com**, **craftbuds.com**

*Photo by Stephanie Purewal*

**Janelle MacKay** of *Emmaline Bags* designs her own line of metal bag hardware and sewing patterns. She lives in Spruce Grove, Alberta, Canada, where she can often be found in a local ice hockey arena sitting with her husband and two adult daughters, screaming, "Shoot!" at her 10-year-old son. The majority of Janelle's day is spent filling bag bling orders, sewing bag prototypes for patterns, shoveling snow, and dreaming of warm places. You can find Janelle's one-of-a-kind bag hardware designs and sewing patterns at *Emmaline Bags*. **emmalinebags.com**, **emmalinebags.blogspot.com**

**RESOURCES**

### Fabric

**Art Gallery Fabrics**   artgalleryfabrics.com

**Birch Fabrics**   birchfabrics.com

**Blend Fabrics**   blendfabrics.com

**Britex Fabrics**   britexfabrics.com

**Cloud9 Fabrics**   cloud9fabrics.com

**FreeSpirit Fabric**   freespiritfabric.com

**Shannon Fabrics**   shannonfabrics.com

**Robert Kaufman Fabrics**   robertkaufman.com

### Sewing Machines and Notions

**Baby Lock**   babylock.com

**ByAnnie's Soft and Stable**   byannie.com

**Clover**   clover-usa.com

**Dritz**   dritz.com

**Emmaline Bags**   emmalinebags.com

**Pellon**   pellonprojects.com